SAVAGERY IN SANDALS

The Gladiators of Ancient Rome

Published by Read & Co. History,
an imprint of Read & Co.

Copyright © 2024 Read & Co. Books

All rights reserved. No portion of this book may be reproduced in any form without the permission of the publisher in writing.

A catalogue record for this book is available from the British Library.

ISBN: 9781528724159

Edited by Gemma Seaton, 2024

Cover Design: Zoe Horn Heywood

Read & Co. is part of Read Books Ltd.
For more information visit www.readandcobooks.co.uk

CONTENTS

THE GLADIATORS OF ANCIENT ROME
An Introduction............................. 5

THE DYING GLADIATOR
A Poem by Lord Byron 9

GLADIATORS
A Dictionary Definition 11

THE STATUE OF THE DYING GLADIATOR
A Poem by Felicia Hemans 21

GLADIATORS
A Slave Sport?.............................. 23

SOURCES OF SUPPLY
An Increase in Demand....................... 29

THE ARENA
Places of Exhibition and Types of Shows........... 31

    Amphitheatres............................ 32

    The Amphitheater at Pompeii................. 43

    The Colosseum........................... 46

    Naumachiae 50

    Beast-Baiting 52

THE SHOW
Advertising, Popularity, Victory, and Defeat........ 56

THE FIGHT
Weapons and Armour 63

GRAFFITI
Gladiators Preserved in Time................... 77

GLADIATOR SCHOOL
Fight or Die................................ 81

FROM ANCIENT SOURCES

GLADIATORS AND WOMEN
Described by Juvenalis and Flaccus 85

    An Elegy to His Mistress. Written by Ovid. 87

GLADIATORS AND SUICIDE
Described by Lucilius. 91

FAMOUS GLADIATORS

A LIST OF GLADIATORS
Mentioned in History. 93

SPARTACUS
A Collection of Writings. 95

    The Revolt of the Gladiators 96

    Spartacus, Crixus, and the Revolt. 100

    Spartacus' Speech 118

COMMODUS
A Collection of Writings. 121

    The Cruelty, Follies and Murder of Commodus . . . 122

PRISCUS AND VERUS
Fragments in History 130

HERMES
Fragments in History 132

BIBLIOGRAPHY. 135

THE GLADIATORS OF ANCIENT ROME

An Introduction

The gladiator holds an almost mythological stance in the modern understanding of Ancient Rome. A brutal spectacle that endured thousands of years, the gladiatorial games were a complex cultural phenomenon that reflected the values, politics, and social dynamics of the Roman Empire. Through the writings of ancient historians, poets, and classical commentators, *Savagery in Sandals* sheds light on the world of the games and the lives of history's most renowned gladiators. This collection of essays and extracts takes a deeper look at the gladiators of the Roman Empire, from the origin of the games, the architecture of the arenas, and the rules of combat, to the individuals who gave their lives for the entertainment of the masses.

Despite the high acclaim of gladiatorial games, the fights, successes, and failures of gladiators were rarely recorded. Gladiators, traditionally slaves and prisoners forced into combat for public amusement, weren't considered significant enough to be remembered due to their low social status. Although there's a lack of written accounts concerning the lives and careers of gladiators, historians have been able to piece fragments of information together from other sources. The Roman graffiti discovered in ancient sites such as Pompeii was crucial in the development of our understanding of gladiator culture, offering unique insights into their lives, relationships, and the public's perception of them. These works of graffiti often featured names, slogans, and drawings, highlighting the fame and admiration some gladiators achieved despite their status. Archaeological findings, such as gladiatorial equipment, amphitheatre remains, and funerary inscriptions, have also provided evidence of the role gladiators played in Roman society.

Encompassing the long history of the Roman Empire, this collection features writings from classical scholars of the nineteenth and twentieth centuries. While a comprehensive approach has been taken, the passages in this volume present the perspectives and prejudices of the authors as well as the audiences they were originally written for. Despite these limitations, *Savagery in Sandals* presents a new perspective on the gladiators of Ancient Rome, from their struggles and triumphs to the enduring legacy of their ruthless profession.

SAVAGERY IN SANDALS

The Gladiators of Ancient Rome

A Retiarius

(Gérôme, 19th century)

THE DYING GLADIATOR

A Poem by Lord Byron

The seal is set—Now welcome thou dread power!
Nameless, yet thus omnipotent, which here
Walk'st in the shadow of the midnight hour,
With a deep awe, yet all distinct from fear;
Thy haunts are ever where the dead walls rear
Their ivy mantles, and the solemn scene
Derives from thee a sense so deep and clear,
That we become a part of what has been,
And grow unto the spot, all seeing but unseen.
And here the buzz of eager nations ran
In murmured pity, or loud roared applause,
As man was slaughtered by his fellow-man.
And wherefore slaughtered? wherefore, but because
Such were the bloody circus' genial laws,
And the imperial pleasure.—Wherefore not?
What matters where we fall to fill the maws
Of worms—on battle plains or listed spot?
Both are but theaters where chief actors rot
I see before me the Gladiator die:
He leans upon his hand—his manly brow
Consents to death, but conquers agony;
And his drooped head sinks gradually low;
And through his side the last drops, ebbing slow
From the red gash, fall heavy, one by one,
Like the first of a thundershower; and now
The arena swims around him—he is gone
Ere ceased the inhuman shout which hailed the wretch who won.
He heard it, but he heeded not—his eyes

SAVAGERY IN SANDALS

Were with his heart, and that was far away
He recked not of the life he lost, nor prize,
But where his rude hut by the Danube lay—
There were his young barbarians all at play;
There was their Dacian mother—he, their sire,
Butchered to make a Roman holiday:
All this rushed with his blood.—Shall he expire,
And unavenged—Arise! ye Goths, and glut your ire!

(Garnett, 1899)

GLADIATORS

A Dictionary Definition

GLADIATORS (from the Latin, *gladius*, sword), professional combatants who fought to the death in Roman public shows. That this form of spectacle, which is almost peculiar to Rome and the Roman provinces, was originally borrowed from Etruria is shown by various indications. On an Etruscan tomb discovered at Tarquinii there is a representation of gladiatorial games; the slaves employed to carry off the dead bodies from the arena wore masks representing the Etruscan Charon; and we learn from Isidore of Seville (*Origines*, x.) that the name for a trainer of gladiators (*lanista*) is an Etruscan word meaning butcher or executioner. These gladiatorial games are evidently a survival of the practice of immolating slaves and prisoners on the tombs of illustrious chieftains, a practice recorded in Greek, Roman and Scandinavian legends, and traceable even as late as the 19th century as the Indian *suttee*. Even at Rome they were for a long time confined to funerals, and hence the older name for gladiators was *bustuarii*; but in the later days of the republic their original significance was forgotten, and they formed as indispensable a part of the public amusements as the theatre and the circus.

The first gladiators are said, on the authority of Valerius Maximus (ii. 4. 7), to have been exhibited at Rome in the Forum Boarium in 264 B.C. by Marcus and Decimus Brutus at the funeral of their father. On this occasion only three pairs fought, but the taste for these games spread rapidly, and the number of combatants grew apace. In 174 Titus Flamininus celebrated his father's obsequies by a three-days' fight, in which 74 gladiators took part. Julius Caesar engaged such extravagant numbers for his aedileship that his political opponents took fright and carried a decree of the senate imposing a certain limit of numbers, but notwithstanding this restriction he was able to exhibit no less than 300 pairs. During the later days of the republic the gladiators were a constant element of danger to the public peace. The more turbulent spirits among the nobility had each his band of gladiators to act as a bodyguard, and the armed troops of Clodius, Milo and Catiline played the same part in Roman history as the armed retainers of the feudal barons or the condottieri of the Italian republics. Under the empire, notwithstanding sumptuary enactments, the passion for the arena steadily increased. Augustus, indeed, limited the shows to two a year, and forbade a praetor to exhibit more than 120 gladiators, yet allusions in Horace (*Sat.* ii. 3. 85) and Persius (vi. 48) show that 100 pairs was the fashionable number for private entertainments; and in the Marmor Ancyranum the emperor states that more than 10,000 men had fought during his reign. Claudius was devoted to this pastime, and would sit from morning till night in his chair of state, descending now and then to the arena to coax or force the reluctant gladiators to resume their bloody work. Under Nero senators and even well-born women appeared as combatants; and Juvenal (viii. 199) has handed down to eternal infamy the descendant of the Gracchi who appeared without disguise as a *retiarius*, and begged his life from the *secutor*, who blushed to conquer one so noble and so vile. Titus, whom his countrymen surnamed the Clement, ordered a show which lasted 100 days; and Trajan, in celebration of his triumph over Decebalus, exhibited 5000 pairs of gladiators. Even women of high birth fought in the arena, and it was not till A.D. 200 that the practice was forbidden by edict. How widely the taste for these sanguinary spectacles extended throughout the Roman provinces is attested by monuments, inscriptions and the remains of vast amphitheatres. From Britain to Syria there was not a town of any size that could not boast its arena and annual games. After Italy, Gaul, North Africa and Spain were most famous for their amphitheatres; and Greece was the only Roman province where the institution never thoroughly took root.

Gladiators were commonly drawn either from prisoners of war, or slaves or criminals condemned to death. Thus in the first class we read of tattooed Britons in their war chariots, Thracians with their peculiar bucklers and scimitars, and Moors from the villages round Atlas, exhibited in the Colosseum. Down to the time of the empire only greater malefactors, such as brigands and incendiaries, were condemned to the arena; but by Caligula, Claudius and Nero this punishment was extended to minor offences, such as fraud and peculation, in order to supply the growing demand for victims. For the first century of the empire it was lawful for masters to sell their slaves as gladiators, but this was forbidden by Hadrian and Marcus Aurelius. Besides these three regular classes, the ranks were recruited by a considerable number of freedmen and Roman citizens who had squandered their estates and voluntarily took the *auctoramentum gladiatorium*, by which for a stated time they bound themselves to the *lanista*. Even men of birth and fortune not seldom entered the lists, either for the pure love of fighting or to gratify the whim of some emperor; and one emperor, Commodus, actually appeared in person in the arena.

Gladiators were trained in schools (*ludi*) owned either by the state or by private citizens, and though the trade of a *lanista* was considered disgraceful, to own gladiators and let them out for hire was reckoned a legitimate branch of commerce. Thus Cicero, in his letters to Atticus, congratulates his friend on the good bargain he had made in purchasing a band, and urges that he might easily recoup himself by consenting to let them out twice. Men recruited mainly from slaves and criminals, whose lives hung on a thread, must have been more dangerous characters than modern galley slaves or convicts; and, though highly fed and carefully tended, they were of necessity subject to an iron discipline. In the school of gladiators discovered at Pompeii, of the sixty-three skeletons buried in the cells many were in irons. But hard as was the gladiators' lot,—so hard that special precautions had to be taken to prevent suicide,—it had its consolations. A successful gladiator enjoyed far greater fame than any modern prize-fighter or athlete. He was presented with broad pieces, chains and jewelled helmets, such as may be seen in the museum at Naples; poets like Martial sang his prowess; his portrait was multiplied on vases, lamps and gems; and high-born ladies contended for his favours. Mixed, too, with the lowest dregs of the city, there must have been many noble barbarians condemned to the vile trade by the hard fate of war. There are few finer characters in Roman history than the Thracian Spartacus, who, escaping with seventy of his comrades from the school of Lentulus at Capua, for three years defied the legions of Rome; and after Antony's defeat at Actium, the only part of his army that remained faithful to his cause were the gladiators whom he had enrolled at Cyzicus to grace his anticipated victory.

There were various classes of gladiators, distinguished by their arms or modes of fighting. The Samnites fought with the national weapons—a large oblong shield, a vizor, a plumed helmet and a short sword. The Thraces had a small round buckler and a dagger curved like a scythe; they were generally pitted against the Mirmillones, who were armed in Gallic fashion with helmet, sword and shield, and were so called from the fish (μορμύλος or μορμύρος) which served as the crest of their helmet. In like manner the Retiarius was matched with the Secutor: the former had nothing on but a short tunic or apron, and sought to entangle his pursuer, who was fully armed, with the cast-net (*jaculum*) that he carried in his right hand; and if successful, he despatched him with the trident (*tridens, fuscina*) that he carried in his left. We may also mention the Andabatae who are generally believed to have fought on horseback and wore helmets with closed vizors; the Dimachaeri of the later empire, who carried a short sword in each hand; the Essedarii, who fought from chariots like the ancient Britons; the Hoplomachi, who wore a complete suit of armour; and the Laquearii, who tried to lasso their antagonists.

Gladiators also received special names according to the time or circumstances in which they exercised their calling. The Bustuarii have already been mentioned; the Catervarii fought, not in pairs, but in bands; the Meridiani came forward in the middle of the day for the entertainment of those spectators who had not left their seats; the Ordinarii fought only in pairs, in the regular way; the Fiscales were trained and supported at the expense of the imperial treasury; the Paegniarii used harmless weapons, and their exhibition was a sham one; the Postulaticii were those whose appearance was asked as a favour from the giver of the show, in addition to those already exhibited.

The shows were announced some days before they took place by bills affixed to the walls of houses and public buildings, copies of which were also sold in the streets. These bills gave the names of the chief pairs of competitors, the date of the show, the name of the giver and the different kinds of combats. The spectacle began with a procession of the gladiators through the arena, after which their swords were examined by the giver of the show. The proceedings opened with a sham fight (*praelusio, prolusio*) with wooden swords and javelins. The signal for real fighting was given by the sound of the trumpet, those who showed fear being driven on to the arena with whips and red-hot irons. When a gladiator was wounded, the spectators shouted *Habet* (he is wounded); if he was at the mercy of his adversary, he lifted up his forefinger to implore the clemency of the people, with whom (in the later times of the republic) the giver left the decision as to his life or death. If the spectators were in favour of mercy, they waved their handkerchiefs; if they desired the death of the conquered gladiator, they turned their thumbs downwards.* The reward

---

* A different account is given by Mayor on Juvenal iii. 36, who says: "Those who wished the death of the conquered gladiator turned their thumbs towards their breasts, as a signal to his opponents to stab him; those who wished him to be spared, turned their thumbs downwards, as a signal for dropping the sword."

of victory consisted of branches of palm, sometimes of money. Gladiators who had exercised their calling for a long time, or such as displayed special skill and bravery, were presented with a wooden sword (*rudis*), and discharged from further service.

Both the estimation in which gladiatorial games were held by Roman moralists, and the influence that they exercised upon the morals and genius of the nation, deserve notice. The Roman was essentially cruel, not so much from spite or vindictiveness as from callousness and defective sympathies. This element of inhumanity and brutality must have been deeply ingrained in the national character to have allowed the games to become popular, but there can be no doubt that it was fed and fostered by the savage form which their amusements took. That the sight of bloodshed provokes a love of bloodshed and cruelty is a commonplace of morals. To the horrors of the arena we may attribute in part, not only the brutal treatment of their slaves and prisoners, but the frequency of suicide among the Romans. On the other hand, we should be careful not to exaggerate the effects or draw too sweeping inferences from the prevalence of this degrading amusement. Human nature is happily illogical; and we know that many of the Roman statesmen who gave these games, and themselves enjoyed these sights of blood, were in every other department of life irreproachable—indulgent fathers, humane generals and mild rulers of provinces. In the present state of society it is difficult to conceive how a man of taste can have endured to gaze upon a scene of human butchery. Yet we should remember that it is not so long since bear-baiting was prohibited in England, and we are only now attaining that stage of morality in respect of cruelty to animals that was reached in the 5th century, in respect of cruelty to men. We shall not then be greatly surprised if hardly one of the Roman moralists is found to raise his voice against this amusement, except on the score of extravagance. Cicero in a well-known passage commends the gladiatorial games as the best discipline against the fear of death and suffering that can be presented to the eye.

SAVAGERY IN SANDALS

Pollice Verso (Thumbs Down)

(Gérôme, 1872)

The younger Pliny, who perhaps of all Romans approaches nearest to our ideal of a cultured gentleman, speaks approvingly of them. Marcus Aurelius, though he did much to mitigate their horrors, yet in his writings condemns the monotony rather than the cruelty. Seneca is indeed a splendid exception, and his letter to Lentulus is an eloquent protest against this inhuman sport. But it is without a parallel till we come to the writings of the Christian fathers, Tertullian, Lactantius, Cyprian and Augustine. In the *Confessions* of the last there occurs a narrative which is worth quoting as a proof of the strange fascination which the games exercised even on a religious man and a Christian. He tells us how his friend Alipius was dragged against his will to the amphitheatre, how he strove to quiet his conscience by closing his eyes, how at some exciting crisis the shouts of the whole assembly aroused his curiosity, how he looked and was lost, grew drunk with the sight of blood, and returned again and again, knowing his guilt yet unable to abstain. The first Christian emperor was persuaded to issue an edict abolishing gladiatorial games (325), yet in 404 we read of an exhibition of gladiators to celebrate the triumph of Honorius over the Goths, and it is said that they were not totally extinct in the West till the time of Theodoric.

Gladiators formed admirable models for the sculptor. One of the finest pieces of ancient sculpture that has come down to us is the "Wounded Gladiator" of the National Museum at Naples. The so-called "Fighting Gladiator" of the Borghese collection, now in the Museum of the Louvre, and the "Dying Gladiator" of the Capitoline Museum, which inspired the famous stanza of *Childe Harold*, have been pronounced by modern antiquaries to represent, not gladiators, but warriors. In this connexion we may mention the admirable picture of Gérome which bears the title, "Ave, Caesar, morituri te salutant."

The attention of archaeologists has been recently directed to the tesserae of gladiators. These tesserae, of which about sixty exist in various museums, are small oblong tablets of ivory or bone, with an inscription on each of the four sides. The first line contains a name in the nominative case, presumably that of the gladiator; the second line a name in the genitive, that of the *patronus* or *dominus*; the third line begins with the letters SP (for *spectatus* = approved), which shows that the gladiator had passed his preliminary trials; this is followed by a day of a Roman month; and in the fourth line are the names of the consuls of a particular year.

(*Encyclopædia Britannica*, 1911)

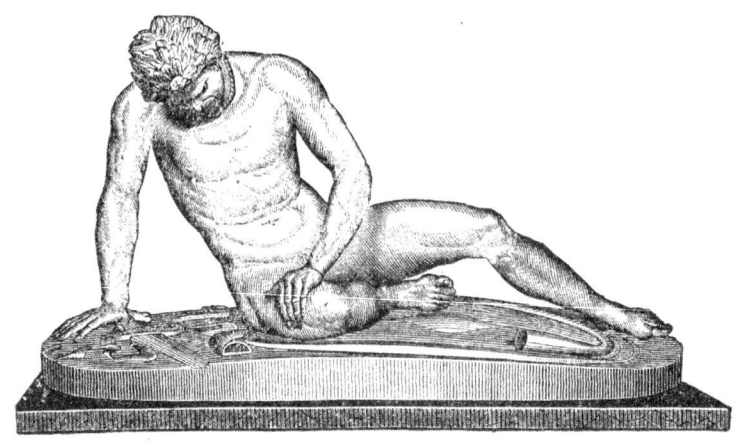

The Statue of the Dying Gladiator

(Yaggy and Haines, 1880)

THE STATUE OF THE DYING GLADIATOR

A Poem by Felicia Hemans

Commanding pow'r! whose hand with plastic art
Bids the rude stone to grace and being start;
Swell to the waving line the polish'd form,
And only want Promethean fire to warm;—
Sculpture, exult! thy triumph proudly see,
The Roman slave immortalized by thee!
No suppliant sighs, no terrors round him wait,
But vanquish'd valor soars above his fate!
In that fix'd eye still proud defiance low'rs,
In that stern look indignant grandeur tow'rs!
He sees e'en death, with javelin barb'd in pain,
A foe *but* worthy of sublime disdain!
Too firm, too lofty, for one parting tear,
A quiv'ring pulse, a struggle, or a fear!

   Oh! fire of soul! by servitude disgrac'd,
   Perverted courage! energy debas'd!
   Lost Rome! thy slave, expiring in the dust,
   Tow'rs far above Patrician rank, august!
   While that proud rank, insatiate, could survey
   Pageants that stain'd with blood each festal day!

Oh! had that arm, which grac'd thy deathful show,
With many a daring feat and nervous blow,
Wav'd the keen sword and rear'd the patriot-shield,
Firm in thy cause, on Glory's laureate field;
Then, like the marble form, from age to age,

SAVAGERY IN SANDALS

His *name* had liv'd in history's brightest page;
While death had but secur'd the victor's crown,
And seal'd the suffrage of deserv'd renown!
That gen'rous pride, that spirit unsubdu'd,
That soul, with honor's high-wrought sense imbu'd,
Had shone, recorded in the song of fame,
A *beam*, as now, a *blemish*, on thy name!

Yet here, so well has art majestic wrought,
Sublimed expression, and ennobled thought;
A dying *Hero* we behold, alone,
And *Mind's bright grandeur* animates the stone!
'Tis not th' Arena's venal champion bleeds,
No! 'tis some warrior, fam'd for matchless deeds!
Admiring rapture kindles into flame,
Nature and art the palm divided claim!
Nature (exulting in her spirit's pow'r,
To rise victorious in the dreaded hour,)
Triumphs, that death and all his shadowy train,
Assail a mortal's constancy—in vain!
And Art, rejoicing in the work sublime,
Unhurt by all the sacrilege of time,
Smiles o'er the marble, her divine control
Moulded to symmetry, and fir'd with soul!

(Hemans, 1812)

GLADIATORS

A Slave Sport?

The mechanic arts, which were formerly in the hands of the clients, were now entirely exercised by slaves: a natural growth of things, for where slaves perform certain labors, such labor will be thought degrading to freemen. The games of the amphitheatre required an immense number of slaves trained for the purpose. Like the slaves in Sicily, the Gladiators of Italy rose in rebellion against their oppressors, (B. C. 73 years.) and under the able generalship of Spartacus, defeated a Roman consular army, and were not subdued until after a struggle of two years, and when 60,000 of them had fallen in battle.

The gladiators, however, were not all slaves. The term is applied to the combatants who fought in the amphitheatre and other places, for the amusement of the Roman people. They are said to have been first exhibited by the Etruscans, and to have had their origin in the custom of killing slaves and captives at the funeral pyres of the deceased. A show of gladiators was called *munus*, and the person who exhibited it, *editor*, or *munerator*, who was honored during the day of exhibition, if a private person, with the insignia of a magistrate.

Gladiators were first exhibited at Rome in B. C. 264, in the Forum Boarium, by Marcus and Decimus Brutus, at the funeral of their father. They were at first confined to public funerals, but afterwards fought at the funerals of most persons of consequence, and even at those of women. Private persons sometimes left a sum of money in their will to pay the expenses of such an exhibition at their funerals. Combats of gladiators were also exhibited at entertainments, and especially at public festivals by the ædiles and other magistrates, who sometimes exhibited immense numbers with a view of pleasing the people. Under the empire, the passions of the Romans for this amusement rose to its greatest height, and the number of gladiators who fought on some occasions appears almost incredible. After Trajan's triumph over the Dacians, there were more than 10,000 exhibited. Gladiators consisted either of captives, slaves and condemned malefactors, or of free-born citizens who fought voluntarily. Of those who were condemned, some were said to be condemned *ad gladium*, in which case they were obliged to be killed within a year, and others *ad ludum*, who might obtain their discharge at the end of three years. Freemen, who became gladiators for hire, were called *auctorati*. Even under the republic, free-born citizens fought as gladiators, but they appear to have belonged only to the lower orders. Under the empire, however, both equites and senators fought in the arena; and even women, which was at length forbidden in the time of Severus. Gladiators were kept in schools, where they were trained by persons called *lanist*. They sometimes were the property of the *lanistæ*, who let them out to persons who wished to exhibit a show of gladiators; but at other times belonged to citizens, who kept them for the purpose of exhibition, and engaged lanistæ to instruct them. The superintendence of the schools which belonged to the emperors, was intrusted to a person of high rank, called curator or procurator. The gladiators fought in these schools with wooden swords. Great attention was paid to their diet in order to increase the strength of their bodies. They were fed with nourishing food; and a great number were trained at Ravenna on account of the salubrity of the place.

 The person who was to exhibit a show of gladiators, published bills containing the numbers and sometimes the names of those who were to fight. When the day came, they were led along the arena in procession, and matched by pairs; and their swords were examined by the exhibitor to see if they were sufficiently sharp.

SAVAGERY IN SANDALS

'Ave, Caesar, morituri te salutant.'

(Hering, 1892)

At first there was a kind of sham battle, called *prelusio*, in which they fought with wooden swords; and afterwards, at the sound of the trumpet, the real battle began. When a gladiator was wounded, the people called out *habet*, or *hoc habet*; and the one who was vanquished, lowered his arms in token of submission. His fate, however, depended upon the audience, who pressed down their thumbs if they wished him to be saved, and turned them up if they wished him to be killed, and ordered him to receive the fatal sword, which they usually did with the greatest firmness. If the life of a vanquished gladiator was spared, he obtained his discharge for that day. In some exhibitions, the lives of the conquered were never spared; but this kind was forbidden by Augustus.

Palms were given to the victorious; money was also sometimes given. Old gladiators, and sometimes those who had fought only for a short time, were discharged from the service by the editor at the request of the people, who presented each of them with a wooden sword. If a person was free before he entered the school, he became free again on his discharge; if he was a slave, he became a slave again. A man, however, who had voluntarily become a gladiator, was always considered to have disgraced himself; and consequently it appears he could not attain the equestrian ranks, if he afterwards acquired sufficient property to entitle him to it.

Shows of gladiators were abolished by Constantine, but appear, notwithstanding, to have been generally exhibited until the time of Honorius, by whom they were finally suppressed.

Gladiators were divided into different classes, according to their arms and different mode of fighting, and other circumstances. One class wore helmets without any aperture for the eyes, so that they were obliged to fight blindfold, and thus excited the mirth of the spectators; another class fought with two swords; another on horseback; another from chariots, like the Gauls and Britons. The laqueators used a noose to catch their adversaries. The meridiani fought in the middle of the day, after the combats with the wild beasts to the morning. The retiarii carried only a three-pointed lance, and a net, which they endeavored to throw over their adversaries, and then attack them with the trident while they were entangled. If he missed his aim in throwing the net, he fled and endeavoured to prepare his net for another cast, while his adversary followed him round the arena in order to kill him before he could make a second attempt. The Thraces were armed with a round shield, and a short sword or dagger. When a gladiator was killed, the attendants, appointed for the purpose, dragged the body out of the arena with iron hooks.

(Blake, 1861)

The Coliseum of Rome

(Yaggy and Haines, 1880)

SOURCES OF SUPPLY

An Increase in Demand

In the early Republic the gladiators were captives taken in war, naturally men practiced in the use of weapons, who thought death by the sword a happier fate than the slavery that awaited them. This always remained the chief source of supply, though it became inadequate as the demand increased. From the time of Sulla training-schools were established in which slaves with or without previous experience in war were fitted for the profession. These were naturally slaves of the most intractable and desperate character. From the time of Augustus criminals were sentenced to the arena (later "to the lions"), but only non-citizens, and these for the most heinous crimes, treason, murder, arson, and the like. Finally in the late Empire the arena became the last desperate resort of the dissipated and prodigal, and these volunteers were numerous enough to be given as a class the name *auctōrātī*.

As the number of the exhibitions increased it became harder and harder to supply the gladiators demanded, for it must be remembered that there were exhibitions in many of the cities of the provinces and in the smaller towns of Italy as well as at Rome. The lines were, therefore, constantly crossed, and thousands died miserably in the arena whom only the most glaring injustice could number in the classes mentioned above. In Cicero's time provincial governors were accused of sending unoffending provincials to be slaughtered in Rome and of forcing Roman citizens, obscure and friendless, of course, to fight in the provincial shows. Later it was common enough to send to the arena men sentenced for the pettiest offenses, when the supply of real criminals had run short, and to trump up charges against the innocent for the same purpose. The persecution of the

Christians was largely due to the demand for more gladiators. So, too, the distinction was lost between actual prisoners of war and peaceful non-combatants; after the fall of Jerusalem all Jews over seventeen years of age were condemned by Titus to work in the mines or fight in the arena. Wars on the border were waged for the sole purpose of taking men who could be made gladiators, and in default of men, children and women were sometimes made to fight.

(Johnston, 1903)

THE ARENA

Places of Exhibition and Types of Shows

During the Republic the combats of gladiators took place sometimes at the grave or in the circus, but regularly in the forum. None of these places was well adapted to the purpose, the grave the least of all. The circus had seats enough, but the *spīna* was in the way and the arena too vast to give all the spectators a satisfactory view of a struggle that was confined practically to a single spot. In the forum, on the other hand, the seats could be arranged very conveniently; they would run parallel with the sides, would be curved around the corners, and would inclose only sufficient space to afford room for the combatants. The inconvenience here was due to the fact that the seats had to be erected before each performance and removed after it, a delay to business if they were constructed carefully and a menace to life if they were put up hastily. These considerations finally led the Romans, as they had led the Campanians half a century before, to provide permanent seats for the *mūnera*, arranged as they had been in the forum, but in a place where they would not interfere with public or private business. To these places for shows of gladiators came in the course of time to be exclusively applied the word *amphitheātrum*, which had been previously given in its correct general sense to any place, the circus for example, in which the seats ran all the way around, as opposed to the theater in which the rows of seats were broken by the stage.

(Johnston, 1903)

Amphitheatres

At an early period, B. C. 263, the practice of compelling human beings to tight for the amusement of spectators was introduced; and twelve years later the capture of several elephants in the first Punic war proved the means of introducing the chase, or rather the slaughter, of wild beasts into the Roman circus. The taste for these spectacles increased of course with its indulgence, and their magnificence with the wealth of the city and the increasing facility and inducement to practice bribery which was offered by the increased extent of provinces subject to Rome. It was not, however, until the last period of the republic, or rather until the domination of the emperors had collected into one channel the tributary wealth which previously was divided among a numerous aristocracy, that buildings were erect ed solely for the accommodation of gladiatorial shows; buildings entirely beyond the compass of a subject's wealth, and in which perhaps the magnificence of imperial Rome is most amply displayed. Numerous examples scattered throughout her empire, in a more or less advanced state of decay, still attest the luxury and solidity of their construction; while at Rome the Coliseum asserts the pre-eminent splendor of the metropolis—a monument surpassed in magnitude by the Pyramids alone, and as superior to them in skill and varied contrivance of design as to other buildings in its gigantic magnitude.

The Greek word, which by a slight alteration of its termination we render amphitheatre, signifies a theatre, or place of spectacles, forming a continuous enclosure, in opposition to the simple theatre, which, as we have said, was semicircular, but with the seats usually continued somewhat in advance of the diameter of the semicircle. The first amphitheatre seems to have been that of Curio, consisting of two movable theatres, which could be placed face to face or back to back, according to the species of amusement for which they were required.

Usually, gladiatorial shows were given in the Forum, and

the chase and combats of wild beasts exhibited in the Circus, where once, when Pompey was celebrating games, some enraged elephants broke through the barrier which separated them from the spectators. This circumstance, together with the unsuitableness of the Circus for such sports, from its being divided into two compartments by the spina, a low wall surmounted by pillars, obelisks, and other ornamental erections, as well as from its disproportionate length, which rendered it ill adapted to afford a general view to all the spectators, determined Julius Caesar, in his dictatorship, to construct a wooden theatre in the Campus Martius, built especially for hunting, " which was called amphitheatre (apparently the first use of the word) because it was encompassed by circular seats without a scene."

The first permanent amphitheatre was built partly of stone and partly of wood, by Statilius Taurus, at the instigation of Augustus, who was passionately fond of these sports, especially of the hunting of rare beasts. This was burnt during the reign of Nero, and though restored, fell short of the wishes of Vespasian, who commenced the vast structure—completed by his son Titus—called the Flavian Amphitheatre, and subsequently the Coliseum. The expense of this building it is said would have sufficed to erect a capital city, and, if we may credit Dion, 9,000 wild beasts were destroyed in its dedication. Eutropius restricts the number to 5,000. When the hunting was over the arena was filled with water, and a sea-fight ensued.

The construction of these buildings so much resembles the construction of theatres, that it will not be necessary to describe them at any great length. Without, they usually presented to the view an oval wall, composed of two or more stories of arcades, supported by piers of different orders of architecture adorned with pilasters or attached pillars. Within, an equal number of stories of galleries gave access to the spectators at different elevations, and the inclined plane of the seats was also supported upon piers and vaults, so that the ground plan presented a number of circular rows of piers, arranged in radii converging to the centre of the arena. A suitable number of doors opened upon the ground floor, and passages from thence, intersecting the circular passages between the piers, gave an easy access to every part of the building. Sometimes a gallery encompassed the whole, and served as a common access to all the stairs which led to the upper stories. This was the case in the amphitheatre at Nismes. Sometimes each staircase had its distinct communication from without: this was the case at Verona.

The arrangement of the seats was the same as in theatres; they were divided horizontally by praecinctiones, and vertically into cunei by staircases. The scene and apparatus of the stage was of course wanting, and its place occupied by an oval area, called arena, from the sand with which it was sprinkled, to absorb the blood shed, and give a firmer footing than that afforded by a stone pavement. It was sunk twelve or fifteen feet below the lowest range of seats, to secure the spectators from injury, and was besides fenced with round wooden rollers turning in their sockets, placed horizontally against the wall, such as the reader may have observed placed on low gates to prevent dogs from climbing over, and with strong nets. In the time of Nero these nets were knotted with amber, and the Emperor Carinus caused them to be made of golden cord or wire. Sometimes, for more complete security, ditches, called euripi, surrounded the arena. This was first done by Caesar, as a protection to the people against the elephants which he exhibited, that animal being supposed to be particularly afraid of water. The arena was sometimes spread with pounded stone. Caligula, in a fit of extravagance, used chrysocolla; and Nero, to surpass him, caused the brilliant red of cinnabar to be mixed with it.

In the centre of the arena was an altar dedicated sometimes to Diana or Pluto, more commonly to Jupiter Latiaris. the protector of Latium, in honor of whom human sacrifices were offered. Passages are to be found in ancient writers, from which it is inferred that the games of the amphitheatre were usually opened by sacrificing a *bestiarius*, one of those gladiators whose profession was to combat wild beasts, in honor of this bloodthirsty deity. Beneath the arena dens are supposed to have been constructed to contain wild beasts.

At the Coliseum numerous underground buildings are said by Fulvius to have existed, which he supposed to be sewers constructed to drain and cleanse the building. Others with more probability have supposed them to be the dens of wild beasts. Immense accommodation was requisite to contain the thousands of animals which were slaughtered upon solemn occasions, but no great provision need have been made to carry off the rain-water which fell upon the six acres comprised within the walls of the building. Others again have supposed them formed to introduce the vast bodies of water by which the arena was suddenly transformed into a lake when imitations of naval battles were exhibited. Doors pierced in the wall which supported the podium communicated with these, or with other places of confinement beneath the part allotted to the audience, which being thrown open, vast numbers of animals could be introduced at once. Vopiscus tells us that a thousand ostriches, a thousand stags, and a thousand boars were thrown into the arena at once by the Emperor Probus. Sometimes, to astonish, and attract by novelty, the arena was converted into a wood. "Probus," says the same author, "exhibited a splendid hunting match, after the following manner: Large trees torn up by the roots were firmly connected by beams, and fixed upright; then earth was spread over the roots, so that the whole circus was planted to resemble a wood, and offered us the gratification of a green scene."

The same order of precedence was observed as at the theatre—senators, knights, and commons having each their appropriate place. To the former was set apart the podium, a broad precinction or platform which ran immediately round the arena. Hither they brought the curule seats or bisellia, described in speaking of the theatres of Pompeii; and here was the suggestus, a covered seat appropriated to the Emperor. It is supposed that in this part of the building there were also seats of honor for the exhibitor of the games and the vestal virgins. If the podium was insufficient for the accommodation of the senators, some of the adjoining seats were taken for their use. Next to the senators sat the knights, who seem here, as in the theatre, to have had fourteen rows set apart for them; and with them sat the civil and military tribunes. Behind were the popularia, or seats of the plebeians. Different tribes had particular cunei allotted to them. There were also some further internal arrangements, for Augustus separated married from unmarried men, and assigned a separate cuneus to youths, near whom their tutors were stationed. Women were stationed in a gallery, and attendants and servants in the highest gallery. The general direction of the amphitheatre was under the care of an officer named *villicus amphitheatri*. Officers called *locarii* attended to the distribution of the people, and removed any person from a seat which he was not entitled to hold. We may notice, as a refinement of luxury, that concealed conduits were carried throughout these buildings, from which scented liquids were scattered over the audience. Sometimes the statues which ornamented them were applied to this purpose, and seemed to sweat perfume through minute holes, with which the pipes that traversed them were pierced. Saffron was the material usually employed for these refreshing showers. The dried herb was infused in wine, more especially in sweet wine. Balsams and the more costly unguents were sometimes employed for the same purpose.

 Another contrivance, too remarkable to be omitted in a general account of amphitheatres, is the awning by which spectators were protected from the overpowering heat of an Italian sun. This was called Velum, or Velarium; and it has afforded matter for a good deal of controversy, how a temporary covering could be extended over the vast areas of these buildings. Something of the kind was absolutely necessary, for the spectacle often lasted for many hours, and when anything extraordinary was expected the people went in crowds before daylight to obtain places, and some even at midnight.

The Campanians first invented the means of stretching awnings over their theatres, by means of cords stretched across the cavea and attached to masts which passed through perforated blocks of stone deeply bedded in the wall. Quintus Catulus introduced them at Rome when he celebrated games at the dedication of the Capitol, B. C. 69. Lentulus Spinther, a contemporary of Cicero, first erected fine linen awnings (carbasina vela). Julius Caesar covered over the whole Forum Romanum, and the Via Sacra, from his own house to the Capitol, which was esteemed even more wonderful than his gladiatorial exhibition. Dio mentions a report that these awnings were of silk, but he speaks doubtfully; and it is scarcely probable that even Caesar's extravagance would have carried him so far. Silk at that time was not manufactured at Rome; and we learn from Vopiscus, that even in the time of Aurelian the raw material was worth its weight in gold. Lucretius, speaking of the effect of colored bodies upon transmitted light, has a fine passage illustrative of the magnificence displayed in this branch of theatrical decoration.

Wool, however, was the most common material, and the velaria made in Apulia were most esteemed, on account of the whiteness of the wool.

Those who are not acquainted by experience with the difficulty of giving stability to tents of large dimensions, and the greater difficulty of erecting awnings, when, on account of the purpose for which they are intended, no support can be applied in the centre, may not fully estimate the difficulty of erecting and managing these velaria. Strength was necessary, both for the cloth itself and for the cords which strained and supported it, or the whole would have been shivered by the first gust of wind, and strength could not be obtained without great weight. Many of our readers probably are not aware, that however short and light a string may be, no amount of tension applied horizontally will stretch it into a line perfectly and mathematically straight. Practically the deviation is imperceptible where the power applied is very large in proportion to the weight and length of the string. Still it exists; and to take a common example, the reader probably never saw a clothes-line stretched out, though neither the weight nor length of the string are considerable, without the middle being visibly lower than the ends. When the line is at once long and heavy, an enormous power is required to suspend it even in a curve between two points; and the amount of tension, and difficulty of finding materials able to withstand it, are the only obstacles to constructing chain bridges which should be thousands, instead of hundreds of feet in length.

In these erections the piers are raised to a considerable height, that a sufficient depth may be allowed for the curve of the chains without depressing the roadway. Ten times—a hundred times the power which was applied to strain them into that shape would not suffice to bring them even so near to a horizontal line but that the most inaccurate and unobservant eye should at once detect the inequality in their level; and the chains themselves would probably give way before such a force as this could be applied to them. The least diameter of the Coliseum is nearly equal in length to the Menai bridge; and if the labor of stretching cords over the one seems small in comparison with that of raising the ponderous chains of the other, we may take into consideration the weight of cloth which those cords supported, and the increase of difficulties arising from the action of the wind on so extensive a surface.

In boisterous weather, as we learn from Martial and other authors, these difficulties were so great that the velum could not be spread. When this was the case the Romans used broad hats, or a sort of parasol, which was called *umbella* or *umbraculum*, from *umbra*, shade. We may add, in conclusion, that Suetonius mentions as one of Caligula's tyrannical extravagances, that sometimes at a show of gladiators, when the sun's heat was most intense, he would cause the awning to be drawn back, and, at the same time, forbid any person to leave the place.

The difficulty of the undertaking has given rise to considerable discussion as to the means by which the Romans contrived to extend the velum at such a height over so great a surface, and to manage it at pleasure. Sailors were employed in the service, for the Emperor Commodus, who piqued himself on his gladiatorial skill, and used to fight in the arena, believing himself mocked by the servile crowd of spectators, when once they hailed him with divine honors, gave order for their slaughter by the sailors who were managing the veils.

Concerning the method of working them no information has been handed down. It is evident, however, that they were supported by masts which rose above the summit of the walls. Near the top of the outer wall of the Coliseum there are 240 consoles, or projecting blocks of stone, in which holes are cut to receive the ends of spars, which ran up through holes cut in the cornice to some height above the greatest elevation of the building. A sufficient number of firm points of support at equal intervals was thus procured; and, this difficulty being overcome, the next was to stretch as tight as possible the larger ropes, upon which the whole covering depended for its stability.

The games to which these buildings were especially devoted were, as we have already hinted, two-fold—those in which wild beasts were introduced, to combat either with each other or with men, and those in which men fought with men. Under the general term of gladiators are comprised all who fought in the arena, though those who pitted their skill against the strength and ferocity of savage animals were peculiarly distinguished by the name of *bestiarii*. In general these unhappy persons were slaves or condemned criminals, who, by adopting this profession, purchased an uncertain prolongation of existence, but freemen sometimes gained a desperate subsistence by thus hazarding their lives; and in the decline of Rome, knights, senators, and even the emperors sometimes appeared in the arena, at the instigation of a vulgar and degrading thirst for popular applause.

(Yaggy and Haines, 1880)

The sight of an ancient amphitheatre is calculated to awake in us emotions of a twofold nature: on the one hand, we cannot suppress our admiration for these edifices, which overpower us by their vast size and majestic proportions; on the other hand, the thought of the spectacles which men came here to witness cannot but fill us with horror and astonishment.

An amphitheatre, properly so called, was a double theatre; Curio's two movable theatres when united formed an ordinary amphitheatre. The largest and most splendid of those which have come down to us is the Colosseum; but there are many others of large dimensions and richly decorated. I need but mention those of Pompeii and Verona. Many of the ancient theatres were of small size; here, on the contrary, what chiefly impresses us is the extent of the amphitheatres, their imposing bulk, and—in the case of some of them the word is in no way an exaggeration—their immensity.

Everyone knows the purposes for which they were used, and the kind of entertainments that was held in them. Were it otherwise, we should find full details in Martial, not so much in his epigrams—though even these contain frequent allusions to topics of this kind—as in a special book which in most editions of his works is placed before all the others, and known as the *De Spectaculis*.

(…)

In the morning it was the custom to exhibit rare beasts, such as antelopes and giraffes, in the arena; then came fights between animals of different species, such as lions and bears, elephants and wild boars, rhinoceroses and leopards. Sometimes the proceedings were varied by pitting wild animals against their tamers. The performance was preceded by processions, including a parade of chariots (*pompa*), this part of the entertainment being regarded by the ascetic school with quite as much distaste as the games in the circus itself. The gladiatorial combats took place in the afternoon. These were not restricted to fencing matches between the participants, fought out to the bitter end; a certain variety was introduced by making the men fight under different rules and with different weapons. The gladiators were followed by the *palmularii* and *scutarii* the *retiarii,* the Thracians, the Myrmidons, etc. Some of the actors were dressed up in historical costumes to represent Ajax, Telamon, etc. Combats between dwarfs and women were also much appreciated by the spectators.

No modern can read the accounts of these famous spectacles without giving the first place in his thoughts to the victims. We can guess but too well what the feelings of the German or barbarian prisoners must have been as they were paraded round in carriages during the "morning spectacle," knowing, as they did, the fate reserved for them in the afternoon. We can understand why they sought to escape, even when suicide, in its most dreadful forms, was the only alternative.* But the testimony of the Christian Fathers confirms what we find recorded elsewhere, namely, that the sight of these doomed spectators proved an irresistible attraction, even to the more indifferent members of the audience, so easily does the craving for new and violent emotions lead men to forget the cruelty involved in their gratification.

The Caesars, in spite of their frequent cruelty, indulged in hobbies of a less gruesome type. When two skilful gladiators killed each other with simultaneous thrusts, Claudius ordered a number of small knives to be made for him out of their sword blades.

It was this same Emperor (he had the reputation of being good-natured but a fool) who, when a part of the spectacle went wrong owing to the fault of one of the officials in charge of the arrangements, ordered the man to be thrown to the

---

* Seneca, *Ep,*, lxx., 17, 20, and 22, tells us that one of them choked himself with a filthy sponge, another pretended to drop asleep and fell with his head under the wheel of a chariot, a third plunged the sword which had been given him to fight with during the *naumachia* into his own breast.

beasts, thus providing the public with an additional and unexpected sensation.*

The craze for going down into the arena and making exhibition of themselves, either as performers or as gladiators, had, as we know, infected even Romans of good family long before the days of Nero and Commodus. Caesar allowed himself to be persuaded into permitting the knights to thus debase themselves, but he begged that no such petition should be presented on behalf of the senators. From the time of Augustus onwards there was scarcely a single spectacle, if Dion may be credited, in which knights and senators did not thus take part.

(Thomas, 1899)

Just when the first amphitheaters, in the special sense of the word, were erected at Rome can not be determined with certainty. The elder Pliny (79 A.D.) tells us that in the year 55 B.C. Caius Scribonius Curio built two wooden theaters back to back, the stages being, therefore, at opposite ends, and gave in them simultaneous theatrical performances in the morning. Then, while the spectators remained in their seats, the two theaters were turned by machinery and brought together face to face, the stages were removed, and in the space they had occupied shows of gladiators were given in the afternoon before the united crowds. This story is all too evidently invented to account for the perfected amphitheater of Pliny's time, which he must have interpreted to mean "a double theater." We are also told that Caesar erected a wooden amphitheater in 46 B.C., but we have no detailed description of it, and no reason to think that it was anything more than a temporary affair. In the year 29 B.C., however, an amphitheater was built by Statilius Taurus, partially at least of stone, that lasted until the great conflagration in the

---

* *Ibid,* An accident of a similar kind happened to one of his *Nomenclatores* (an official whose duty it was to announce visitors), who was thrown into the arena, toga and all.

reign of Nero (64 A.D.). Nero himself had previously erected one of wood in the Campus. Finally, just before the end of the first century of our era, was completed the *amphitheātrum Flāvium*, later known as the *colossēum* or *colisēum*, which was large enough and durable enough to make forever unnecessary the erection of other similar structures in the city.

The Amphitheater at Pompeii

The essential features of an amphitheater may be most easily understood from the ruins of the one at Pompeii, erected about 75 B.C., almost half a century before the first permanent structure of the sort at Rome, and the earliest known to us from either literary or monumental sources.

Exterior of Amphitheater at Pompeii

It will be seen at once that the arena and most of the seats lie in a great hollow excavated for the purpose, thus making sufficient for the exterior a low wall of hardly more than ten to thirteen feet in height. Even this wall was necessary on only two sides, as the amphitheater was built in the southeast corner of the city and its south and east sides were bounded by the city walls. The shape is elliptical, the major axis being 444 feet, the minor 342. The arena occupies the middle space. It was encircled by thirty-five rows of seats arranged in three divisions, the lowest (*īnfima* or *īma cavea*) having five rows, the second (*media cavea*) twelve, and the highest (*summa cavea*) eighteen. A broad terrace ran around the amphitheater at the height of the topmost row of seats. Access to this terrace was given from without by the double stairway on the west, and by single stairways next the city walls on the east and south (*10 on 'Plan of Arena' image*). Between the terrace and the top seats was a gallery, or row of boxes, each about four feet square, probably for women. Beneath the boxes persons could pass from the terrace to the seats. The amphitheater had seating capacity for about 20,000 people. The arena is shown in image above. It was an ellipse with axes of 228 and 121 feet. Around it ran a wall a little more than six feet high, on a level with the top of which were the lowest seats. For the protection of the spectators when wild animals were shown, a grating of iron bars was put up on the top of the arena wall.

INTERIOR OF AMPHITHEATER AT POMPEII

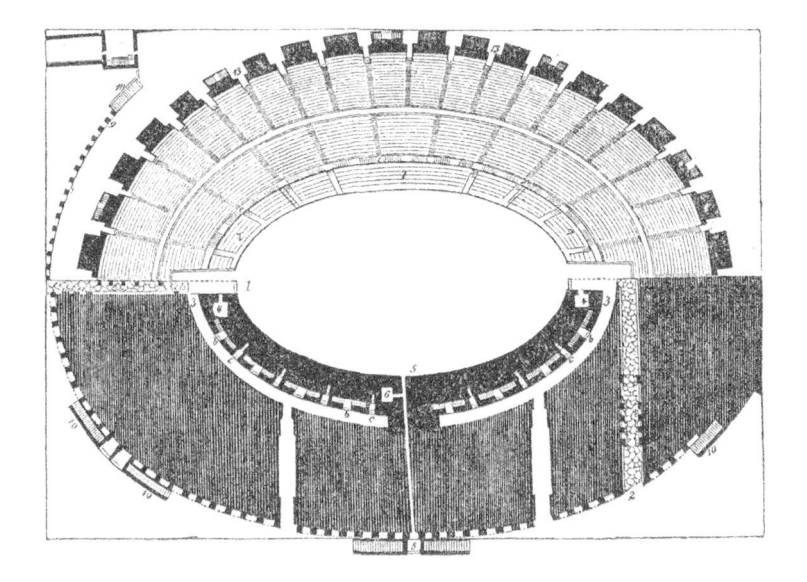

PLAN OF ARENA IN AMPHITHEATER AT POMPEII

Access to the arena and to the seats of the *cavea īma* and the *cavea media* was given by the two underground passageways, *1* and *2* in image above, of which *2* turns at right angles on account of the city wall on the south. From the arena ran also a third passage, *5*, low and narrow, leading to the *porta Libitinēnsis*, through which the bodies of the dead were dragged with ropes and hooks. Near the mouths of these passages were small chambers or dens, marked *4, 4, 6*, the purposes of which are not known. The floor of the arena was covered with sand, as in the circus, but in this case to soak up the blood as well as to give a firm footing to the gladiators.

Of the part of this amphitheater set aside for the spectators the *cavea īma* only was supported upon artificial foundations. All the other seats were constructed in sections as means were obtained for the purpose, the people in the meantime finding places for themselves on the sloping banks as in the early theaters. The *cavea īma* was strictly not supplied with seats all the way around, a considerable section on the east and west sides being arranged with four low, broad ledges of stone, rising one above the other, on which the members of the city council could place the seats of honor to which their rank entitled them. In the middle of the section on the east the lowest ledge is made of double width for some ten feet; this was the place set apart for the giver of the games and his friends. In the *cavea media* and the *cavea summa* the seats were of stone resting on the bank of earth. It is probable that all the places in the lowest section were reserved for people of distinction, that seats in the middle section were sold to the well-to-do, and that admission was free to the less desirable seats of the highest section.

(Johnston, 1903)

The Colosseum

The Flavian amphitheater is the best known of all the buildings of ancient Rome, because to a larger extent than others it has survived to the present day. For our purpose it is not necessary to give its history or to describe its architecture; it will be sufficient to compare its essential parts with those of its modest prototype in Pompeii. The latter was built in the outskirts of the city, in a corner in fact of the city walls; the coliseum lay almost in the center of Rome, the most generally accessible of all the public buildings. The interior of the Pompeian structure was reached through two passages and by three stairways only, while eighty numbered entrances made it easy for the Roman multitudes to find their appropriate places in the coliseum. Much of the earlier amphitheater was underground; all of the corresponding parts of the coliseum were above the level of the street, the walls rising to a height of nearly 160 feet. This gave opportunity for the same architectural magnificence that had distinguished the Roman theater from that of the Greeks. The general effect is shown in the image below, an exterior view of the ruins as they exist today.

SAVAGERY IN SANDALS

Exterior of the Colosseum

Interior of the Colosseum

The form is an ellipse with axes of 620 and 513 feet, the building covering nearly six acres of ground. The arena is also an ellipse, its axes measuring 287 and 180 feet. The width of the space appropriated for the spectators is, therefore, 166½ feet all around the arena. It will be noticed, too, that subterranean chambers were constructed under the whole building, including the arena. These furnished room for the regiments of gladiators, the dens of wild beasts, the machinery for the transformation scenes that Gibbon has described in his twelfth chapter, and above all for the vast number of water and drainage pipes that made it possible to turn the arena into a lake at a moment's notice and as quickly to get rid of the water. The wall that surrounded the arena was fifteen feet high with the side faced with rollers and defended like the one at Pompeii with a grating or network of metal above it. The top of the wall was level with the floor of the lowest range of seats, called the *podium* as in the circus, and this had room for two or at the most three rows of marble thrones. These were for the use of the emperor and the imperial family, the giver of the games, the magistrates, senators, Vestal virgins, ambassadors of foreign states, and other persons of consequence.

The arrangement of the seats with the method of reaching them is shown in the sectional plan. The seats were arranged in three tiers (*maeniāna*) one above the other, separated by broad passageways and rising more steeply the farther they were from the arena, and were crowned by an open gallery. In the plan the *podium* is marked A. Twelve feet above it begins the first *maeniānum*, B, with fourteen rows of seats reserved for members of the equestrian order. Then came a broad *praecīnctiō* and after it the second *maeniānum*, C, intended for ordinary citizens. Back of this was a wall of considerable height and above it the third *maeniānum*, D, supplied with rough wooden benches for the lowest classes, foreigners, slaves, and the like. The row of pillars along the front of this section made the distant view all the worse. Above this was an open gallery, E, in which women found an unwelcome place.

SAVAGERY IN SANDALS

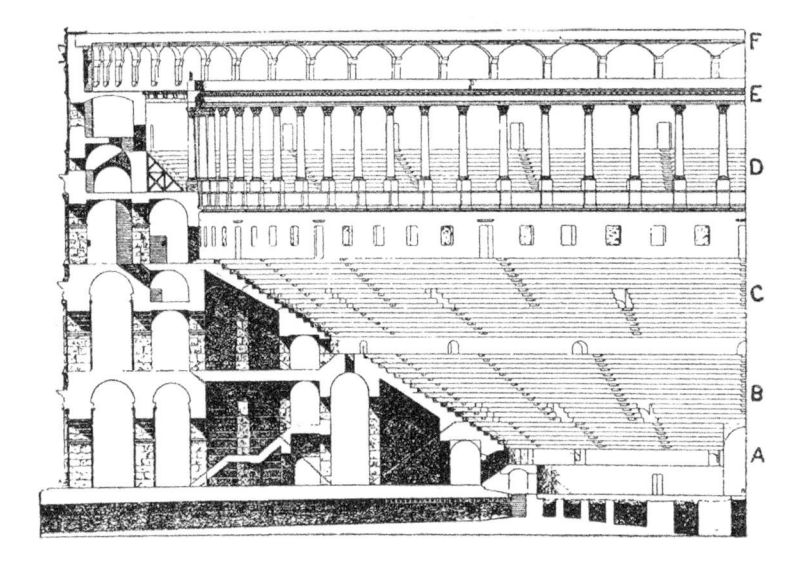

SECTION OF THE COLOSSEUM

No other seats were open to them unless they were of sufficient distinction to claim a place upon the *podium*. At the very top of the outside wall was a terrace, F, in which were fixed masts to support the awnings that gave protection against the sun. The seating capacity of the coliseum is said to have been 80,000, and it had standing room for 20,000 more.

(Johnston, 1903)

Naumachiae

The naumachia was a special form of gladiatorial combat in which fleets manned by trained gladiators, condemned criminals, or prisoners of war met on an artificial or natural lake and enacted scenes of naval warfare, generally reproductions of historical sea-fights. The first recorded exhibition of this sort was given by Julius Caesar in 46 B.C.; an artificial lake was dug on the right bank of the Tiber, in communication with the river, and two fleets, representing those of Tyre and Egypt, manned by 4,000 rowers and 2,000 fighting men, were pitted against each other. This lake was, however, soon afterwards filled up; and the first permanent *naumachia* (in the sense of a lake for sea-fights, for which in pure Latin *navale stagnum* is used) was the work of Augustus. It has been shown by Huelsen that this was in the northerly part of the modern Trastevere, at the foot of the Vatican. It was fed by the aqua *Alsietina*, and stood in a park called the *Nemus Caesarum* in honour of Gaius and Lucius Caesar, the grandsons of Augustus.

It was constructed for the games given by Augustus in 2 B.C. at the dedication of the temple of Mars Ultor, and was 1,800 Roman feet long and 1,200 feet broad. The naumachia then exhibited was a reproduction of the battle of Salamis, and 3,000 combatants (exclusive of rowers) took part in it. It was used several times during the first century A.D., notably by Nero and Titus,[*] but afterwards fell into disuse, so that only its ruins were visible in the time of Dio Cassius. This was perhaps because a second *naumachia* had been built in the region between the mausoleum of Hadrian and the Vatican, remains of which were brought to light in the eighteenth century; this is no doubt that

---

[*] Titus boarded over the *naumachia Augusti* and gave gladiatorial shows in it on two days, reserving the third for a representation of the battle of Salamis, in which an artificial island was captured by the 'Athenians'.

which is ascribed by the historians to Domitian.

Naumachiae were at times held in the *arena* of the amphitheatre, which was specially flooded for the purpose. Thus Nero exhibited *naumachiae* both at the inauguration of his wooden amphitheatre in A.D. 57 and again in A.D. 64; and Titus caused the battle of the Corcyrean and Corinthian fleets to be represented at the opening of the Flavian amphitheatre in A.D. 80. Domitian also gave a *naumachia* in the Colosseum; but it is a mistake to suppose that this was a regular practice. In fact, *naumachiae* are seldom heard of after the first century A.D.; the last of which we have any knowledge (and this is merely conjectural) was celebrated by Philip the Arabian on the occasion of his *ludi saeculares*.

The most famous *naumachia* in the history of the Empire was that given by Claudius on the Fucine Lake as a prelude to the opening of the *emissarium*. The fleets, fifty on each side, consisting of triremes and quadriremes, represented the naval forces of Rhodes and Sicily, and were manned by 19,000 condemned criminals, prevented from escaping by a barricade of rafts on which were stationed troops of horse and foot, and engines of war. The signal was given by a silver Triton, which blew a horn worked by mechanism; but the criminals at first refused to fight, though they afterwards did so 'with the spirit of brave men', as Tacitus tells us.

(Jones, 1912)

BEAST-BAITING

Amongst the shows given in the Circus by which generals or magistrates sought to win popularity with the Roman people were wild-beast hunts. As early as 250 B.C., L. Caecilius Metellus exhibited 120 elephants in the Circus when he triumphed over the Carthaginians; but these were not, it seems, hunted, and the first *venatio* in the proper sense was given by M. Fulvius Nobilior, the conqueror of the Aetolian League, in 186 B.C., when lions and panthers were brought into the arena in such numbers that Livy (xxxix. 22) compares the magnificence of the spectacle with those seen in his own time. Seventeen years later sixty-three panthers and leopards, together with forty bears and several elephants, were exhibited by the curule aediles P. Cornelius Scipio Nasica and P. Cornelius Lentulus. For a century and more these African beasts were the only ones which made their appearance in the Circus beside the stags, boars, and bears of Europe; but in the closing years of the Republic the ambition of wealthy aspirants to political distinction caused search to be made farther afield. In 58 B.C. the curule aedile, M. Aemilius Scaurus, exhibited a hippopotamus and five crocodiles, for which a temporary reservoir was set up. Three years later Pompey showed a rhinoceros, an anthropoid ape, and a Gallic lynx. Finally, in 46 B.C., the giraffe was seen for the first time at the games which accompanied Julius Caesar's triumph. Nor was it only the rarity of the animals exhibited which made these shows historic. The numbers given by the historians are barely credible. At Pompey's games 500 (or 600) lions, 410 leopards and panthers, and 17 elephants were shown; Caesar brought together 40 elephants and 400 lions. Naturally these figures were surpassed under the Empire. Augustus tells us in the *Monumentum Ancyranum* that 3,500 African beasts were killed at his shows; and he enjoyed the distinction of being the first to exhibit the tiger at the games given in 11 B.C. at the dedication of the theatre of Marcellus. This was but a single specimen shown in a cage; but Claudius was able to show four, and Domitian, Antoninus Pius, and Septimius Severus exhibited a larger number. The emperors also showed various species of the antelope, and probably the zebra, from Africa, as well as elks and bison from Central and Northern Europe.

Under the Empire the number of beasts exhibited on important occasions was enormous. At the dedication of the Colosseum in A.D. 80, 9,000 tame and wild beasts were killed, and at the shows of A.D.107, given in honour of Trajan's second Dacian triumph, 11,000 were slaughtered.

Originally these exhibitions were held in the Circus, but Julius Caesar, and after him Statilius Taurus, built wooden amphitheatres specially for this purpose; and after the construction of the Colosseum *venationes* were regularly held there, though the Circus was occasionally used. The shows were of different kinds. The rarer beasts were often merely paraded for the inspection of the audience; but as a rule they were either hunted or baited by trained men (*venatores*), or else were permitted to devour condemned criminals (*bestiarii*), who were exposed in the arena unarmed (or insufficiently armed), or even tied to stakes.

This punishment was commonly inflicted on Christians, and, under the later Empire, was reserved for criminals of the lower orders. We have representations of these combats on many works of art.

One of the ivory diptychs* shows the *bestiarii* taking advantage of the turnstiles which enabled them to evade the charge of the animal; on the other we see them vaulting over railings or swung

---

* The diptych was formed of two tablets of ivory or bone hinged together, and was presented by consuls and other magistrates to their friends with an invitation to attend the shows which they gave on assuming office.

in baskets from a pole.* At other times the beasts were made to fight with each other, e.g. a rhinoceros with an elephant, or a bull with a bear. Others, again, were trained to perform tricks in the arena—such as the lions, which (in Domitian's time) were taught to catch hares and bring them to their master, or the elephants, which, we are told, could write in Greek or Latin.

(Jones, 1912)

---

* These devices for the protection of the *bestiarius*, which were introduced in Christian times, are mentioned by Cassiodorus, the minister of Theodoric and his successors.

SAVAGERY IN SANDALS

The Christian Martyrs; or, The Last Prayer

(Hering, 1892)

THE SHOW

Advertising, Popularity, Victory, and Defeat

The games were advertised in advance by means of notices painted on the walls of public and private houses, and even on the tombstones that lined the approaches to the towns and cities. Some are worded in very general terms, announcing merely the name of the giver of the games with the date:

A • Svetti • Certi
AEDILIS • FAMILIA • GLADIATORIA • PUGNAB • POMPEIS
pr • k • Jvnias • Venatio • ET • VELA • ERUNT*

Others promise in addition to the awnings that the dust will be kept down in the arena by sprinkling. Sometimes when the troop was particularly good the names of the gladiators were announced in pairs as they would be matched together, with details as to their equipment, the school in which each had been trained, the number of his previous battles, etc. To such a notice on one of the walls in Pompeii some one added after the show the result of each combat.

The following is a specimen only of this announcement:

---

* "On the last day of May the gladiators of the Aedile Aulus Suettius Certus will fight at Pompeii. There will also be a hunt and the awnings will be used."

MVNVS • N ... • IV • III
PRID • IDVS • IDIBVS • MAIS

T	M	O	T
v. PVGNAX • NER • III		*v.* CYCNVS • IVL • VIII	
p. MVRRANVS • NER • III		*m.* ATTICVS • IVL • XIV	

The letters in italics before the names of the gladiators were added after the exhibition by some interested spectator, and stand for *vīcit*, *periit*, and *missus* ("beaten, but spared").* Other announcements added to such particulars as those given above the statement that other pairs than those mentioned would fight each day, this being meant to excite the curiosity and interest of the people.

The day before the exhibition a banquet (*cēna lībera*) was given to the gladiators and they received visits from their friends and admirers. The games took place in the afternoon. After the *ēditor mūneris* had taken his place, the gladiators marched in procession around the arena, pausing before him to give the famous greeting: *moritūrī tē salūtant*. All then retired from the arena to return in pairs according to the published programme. The show began with a series of sham combats, the *prōlūsiō*, with blunt weapons. When the people had had enough of this the trumpets gave the signal for the real exhibition to begin. Those reluctant to fight were driven into the arena with whips or hot iron bars. If one of the combatants was clearly overpowered without being actually killed, he might appeal for mercy by holding up his finger to the *ēditor*. It was customary to refer the plea to the people, who waved cloths or napkins to show that they

---

* "The games of N . . . from the 12th to the 15th of May. The Thracian Pugnax, of the gladiatorial school of Nero, who has fought three times will be matched against the *murmillō* Murranus, of the same school and the same number of fights. The *hoplomachus* Cycnus, from the school of Julius Caesar, who has fought eight times will be matched with the Thracian Atticus of the same school and of fourteen fights."

wished it to be granted, or pointed their thumbs downward as a signal for death. The gladiator who was refused release (*missiō*) received the death blow from his opponent without resistance. Combats where all must fight to the death were said to be *sine missiōne*, but these were forbidden by Augustus. The body of the dead man was dragged away through the *porta Libitinēnsis*, sand was sprinkled or raked over the blood, and the contests were continued until all had fought.

D • M • et • Memoriae
aeternae • HYLATIS
dymachaero • sive
assidario • p • VII • rv • I
ERMAIS • conivx
conivgi • karissimo
p • c • et • s • as • d

Inscription on Tomb of a Gladiator

"To the Gods Manes and the lasting memory of Hylas, a dimachaerus or essedarius of seven victories and head trainer. His wife Ermais erected this monument to her beloved husband and dedicated it, reserving the usual rights."

On the appointed day the gladiators marched in procession with much ceremony into the amphitheatre. They then separated into pairs, as they had been previously matched. An engraving on the wall of the amphitheatre at Pompeii seems to represent the beginning of a combat. In the middle stands the arbiter of the fight, marking out with a long stick the space for the combatants. On his right stands a gladiator only half armed, to whom two others are bringing a sword and helmet. On the left another gladiator, also only partly armed, sounds the trumpet for the commencement of the fight; whilst behind him two companions, at the foot of one of the Victories which enclose the scene, are preparing his helmet and shield.

At first, however, they contended only with staves, called *rudes*, or with blunted weapons; but when warmed and inspirited by the pretense of battle, they changed their weapons, and advanced at the sound of trumpets to the real strife. The conquered looked to the people or to the emperor for life; his antagonist had no power to grant or to refuse it; but if the spectators were dissatisfied and gave the signal of death, he was obliged to become the executioner of their will. This signal was the turning down the thumbs; as is well known. If any showed signs of fear, their death was certain; if on the other hand they waited the fatal stroke with intrepidity, the people generally relented. But fear and want of spirit were of very rare occurrence, insomuch that Cicero more than once proposed the principle of honor which actuated gladiators as an admirable model of constancy and courage, by which he intended to animate himself and others to suffer everything in defence of the commonwealth.

(Yaggy and Haines, 1880)

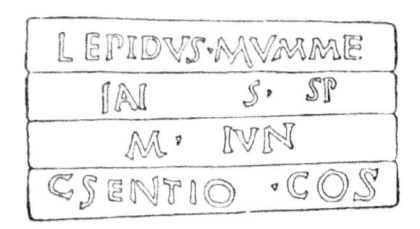

```
L EPIDVS·MVMME
 IAI       S·  SP
   M·   IVN
 CSENTIO   ·COS
```

TESSERA GLADIATORIA

Before making his first public appearance the gladiator was technically called a *tīrō*. After his first victory he received a token of wood or ivory (Fig. 168), which had upon it his name and that of his master or trainer, a date, and the letters SP, SPECT, SPECTAT, or SPECTAVIT, meaning perhaps *populus spectāvit*. When after many victories he had proved himself to be the best of his class, or second best, in his *familia*, he received the title of *prīmus*, or *secundus*, *pālus*. When he had won his freedom he was given a wooden sword (*rudis*). From this the titles *prīma rudis* and *secunda rudis* seem to have been given to those who were afterwards employed as training masters (*doctōrēs*) in the schools. The rewards given to famous gladiators by their masters and backers took the form of valuable prizes and gifts of money. These may not have been so generous as those given to the *aurīgae*, but they were enough to enable them to live in luxury the rest of their lives. The class of men, however, who followed this profession probably found their most acceptable reward in the immediate and lasting notoriety that their strength and courage brought them. That they did not shrink from the *īnfamia* that the profession entailed is shown by the fact that they did not try to hide their connection with the amphitheater. On the contrary, their gravestones record their classes and the number of their victories, and have often cut upon them their likenesses with the *rudis* in their hands.

(Johnston, 1903)

In the fights of gladiators, the people disapproved of that gladiator who aimed too constantly at the vital parts of his adversary, so as to make the combat short.

Palma lemniscata is a palm branch (i.e. a token of victory,) given to a gladiator or general when the victory was very remarkable.

(Cicero and Yonge, 1851)

The Romans' love of excitement made the exhibitions immediately and immensely popular. At the first exhibition mentioned above, that in honor of Brutus Pera, three pairs of gladiators only were shown, but in the three that followed the number of pairs rose in order to twenty-two, twenty-five, and sixty. By the time of Sulla politicians had found in the *mūnera* the most effective means to win the favor of the people, and vied with one another in the frequency of the shows and the number of the combatants. Besides this, the same politicians made these shows a pretext for surrounding themselves with bands of bravos and bullies, all called gladiators whether destined for the

SAVAGERY IN SANDALS

arena or not, with which they started riots in the streets, broke up public meetings, overawed the courts and even directed or prevented the elections. Caesar's preparations for an exhibition when he was canvassing for the aedileship (65 B.C.) caused such general fear that the senate passed a law limiting the number of gladiators that a private citizen might employ, and he was allowed to exhibit only 320 pairs. The bands of Clodius and Milo made the city a slaughterhouse in 53 B.C., and order was not restored until late in the following year when Pompey as "sole consul" put an end to the battle of the bludgeons with the swords of his soldiers. During the Empire the number actually exhibited almost surpasses belief. Augustus gave eight *munera*, in which no less than ten thousand men fought, but these were distributed through the whole period of his reign. Trajan exhibited as many in four months only of the year 107 A.D., in celebration of his conquest of the Dacians. The first Gordian, emperor in 238 A.D., gave *munera* monthly in the year of his aedileship, the number of pairs running from 150 to 500. These exhibitions did not cease until the fifteenth century of our era.

(Johnston, 1903)

A WOUNDED GLADIATOR

The bodies of the slain were dragged with a hook or on a cart through a gate called Libitinensis, the Gate of Death. The victor was rewarded with a sum of money, contributed by the spectators or bestowed from the treasury, or a palm-branch, or a garland of palm ornamented with colored ribbons—ensigns of frequent occurrence in ancient monuments. Those who survived three years were released from this service, and sometimes one who had given great satisfaction was enfranchised on the spot. This was done by presenting the staff (*rudis*) which was used in preluding to the combat; on receiving which, the gladiator, if a freeman, recovered his liberty; if a slave, he was not made free, but was released from the obligation of venturing his life any further in the arena.

(Yaggy and Haines, 1880)

THE FIGHT

Weapons and Armour

Gladiators fought usually in pairs, man against man, but sometimes in masses (*gregātim*, *catervātim*). In early times they were actually soldiers, captives taken in war, and fought naturally with the weapons and equipment to which they were accustomed. When the professionally trained gladiators came in, they were given the old names, and were called Samnites, Thracians, etc., according to their arms and tactics. In much later times victories over distant peoples were celebrated with combats in which the weapons and methods of war of the conquered were shown to the people of Rome; thus, after the conquest of Britain *essedāriī* exhibited in the arena the tactics of chariot fighting which Caesar had described generations before in his Commentaries. It was natural enough, too, for the people to want to see different arms and different tactics tried against each other, and so the Samnite was matched against the Thracian, the heavy armed against the light armed. This became under the Empire the favorite style of combat. Finally when people had tired of the regular shows, novelties were introduced that seem to us grotesque; men fought blindfold (*andabatae*), armed with two swords (*dimachaerī*), with the lasso (*laqueatōrēs*), with a heavy net (*rētiāriī*), and there were battles of dwarfs and of dwarfs with women. Of these the *rētiārius* became immensely popular. He carried a huge net in which he tried to entangle his opponent, always a *secūtor* (see below), despatching him with a dagger if the throw was successful. If unsuccessful he took to flight while preparing his net for another throw, of if he had lost his net tried to keep his opponent off with a heavy three-pronged spear (*fuscina*), his only weapon beside the dagger.

RETIARIUS AND SECUTOR

The armor and weapons used in these combats are known from pieces found in various places and from paintings and sculpture, but we are not always able to assign them to definite classes of gladiators. The oldest class was that of the Samnites. They had belts, thick sleeves on the right arm (*manica*), helmets with visors, shown in image below, greaves on the left leg, short swords, and the long shield (*scūtum*). Under the Empire the name Samnite was gradually lost and gladiators with equivalent equipment were called *hoplomachī* (heavy armed), when matched against the lighter armed Thracians, and *secūtōrēs*, when they fought with the *rētiāriī*.

The Thracians had much the same equipment as the Samnites, the mark of distinction being the small shield (*parma*) in place of the *scūtum* and, to make up the difference, greaves on both legs. They carried a curved sword.

SAVAGERY IN SANDALS

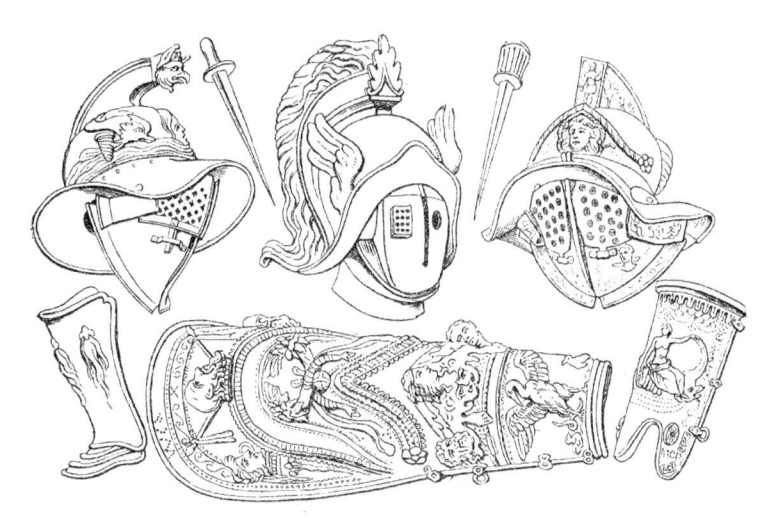

Weapons of Gladiators

The Gauls were heavy armed, but we do not know how they were distinguished from the Samnites. In later times they were called *murmillōnēs*, from an ornament on their helmets shaped like a fish (*mormyr*). The rētiāriī had no defensive armor except a leather protection for the shoulder. Of course the same man might appear by turns as Samnite, Thracian, etc., if he was skilled in the use of the various weapons.

Helmets of Gladiators

(Johnston, 1903)

Gladiators were divided, according to the fashion of their armor and offensive weapons, into classes, known by the names of Thrax, Samnis, Myrmillo, and many others, of which a mere catalogue would be tedious, and it would be the work of a treatise to ascertain and describe their distinctive marks.

THRAEX

Another group consists of four figures. Two are *secutores*, followers, the other two, *retiarii*, net men, armed only with a trident and net, 'with which they endeavored to entangle their adversary, and then dispatch him. These classes, like the Thrax and Myrmillo, were usual antagonists, and had their name from the secutor following the retiarius, who eluded the pursuit until he found an opportunity to throw his net to advantage. Nepimus, one of the latter, live times victorius, has fought against one of the former, whose name is lost, but who had triumphed six times in different combats. He has been less fortunate in this battle. Nepimus has struck him in the leg, the thigh, and the left arm; his blood runs, and in vain he implores mercy from the spectators. As the trident with which Nepimus is armed is not a weapon calculated to inflict speedy and certain death, the secutor Hyppolitus performs this last office to his comrade.

The condemned wretch bends the knee, presents his throat to the sword and throws himself forward to meet the blow, while

SAVAGERY IN SANDALS

Nepimus, his conqueror, pushes him, and seems to insult the last moments of his victim. In the distance is the retiarius, who must fight Hyppolitus in his turn.

ASKING PARDON.   NOT GRANTED.

The secutores have a very plain helmet, that their adversary may have little or no opportunity of pulling it off with the net or trident; the right arm is clothed in armor, the left bore a *clypeus*, or large round shield; a sandal tied with narrow bands forms the covering for their feet. They wear no body armor, no covering but a cloth round the waist, for by their lightness and activity alone could they hope to avoid death and gain the victory. The retiarii have the head bare, except a fillet bound round the hair; they have no shield, but the left side is covered with a demi-cuiarass, and the left arm protected in the usual manner, except that the shoulder-piece is very high. They wear the caliga, or low boot common to the Roman soldiery, and bear the trident; but the net with which they endeavored to envelop their adversaries is nowhere visible. This bas-relief is terminated by the combat between a light-armed gladiator and a Samnite. This last beseeches the spectators to save him, but it appears from the action of the principal figure that this is not granted. The conqueror looks towards the steps of the amphitheatre; he has seen the fatal signal, and in reply prepares himself to strike.

(Yaggy and Haines, 1880)

The institution which to modern minds appears the darkest blot on Roman civilization was not of native origin in Rome. According to tradition, the practice of pitting slaves or prisoners of war against each other in mortal combat was introduced into Italy by the Etruscans at the funeral games of their nobles; and there are representations on their sepulchral urns which confirm the truth of this statement. It may well be that the Romans borrowed this custom directly from their northern neighbours; at any rate, the first recorded example of a gladiatorial show in Rome was an exhibition of three duels between pairs of swordsmen at the funeral games (*ludi funebres*) of Brutus Pera, celebrated in 264 B.C. by his two sons; and for a full century and a half after this date gladiators were only exhibited at such private celebrations, the chief of which were the games celebrated by Flamininus, the liberator of the Greeks, at his father's obsequies. Notwithstanding, there is some ground for the view that the Campanians played an even more important part than the Etruscans in the history of gladiatorial shows. It was doubtless from the Etruscans, whose influence extended in early times as far south as the Bay of Naples, and was predominant until the close of the fifth century B.C., that the Oscans learnt the practice; but they carried it even further than their teachers, for we hear that gladiators were shown not only at funeral games but also at banquets, and it has already been pointed out that the amphitheatre itself is in all probability a Campanian invention. Livy tells us that after a victory gained by the Romans and their Campanian allies over the Samnites in 310 B.C., the Campanians used the arms of their fallen enemies to equip their gladiators, whom they called 'Samnites'; and whether this story be true or not, it accords well with the fact that the 'Samnite' was the earliest and for some time almost the only type of gladiator exhibited in Rome. The Samnite armour, as described by Livy in the passage quoted, and represented on monuments such as the wall-paintings of Paestum, was certainly copied in essentials from the equipment of the 'Samnite' gladiator.

TOMB-RELIEF OF M. ANTONIUS EXOCLIUS, A THRAEX
(from a drawing in the Royal Library at Windsor).

He was armed with the sword and *scutum*, and wore a helmet (*galea*) with side-feathers (*pinnae*) and high crest (*crista*), and a greave or leg-guard (*ocrea*) on the left leg only—agreeing so far with the description of Livy. He wore no cuirass or tunic, however, but only a loin-cloth or drawers (*subligaculum*) girt about the waist with a belt (*balteus*), and an armguard formed of strips of leather (*manica*) upon his right arm. It has been observed that the name *Samnes* is never used by post-Augustan writers (it is last used by Horace); but the type certainly continued to exist, for Juvenal mentions the *balteus et manicae et cristae crurisque sinistri dimidium tegimen*, and we find them represented on many monuments of the Empire. The explanation is not far to seek. In Republican times a duel of Samnite against Samnite contented the public taste; under the Empire more variety was demanded; and the swordsmen, under fresh names, were pitted against fresh antagonists. Thus the *(h)oplomachus*, often mentioned in literature and inscriptions, is nothing but the *Samnes* of earlier times; but his adversary is almost always the 'Thracian', to be described presently. Moreover, the *secutor*, first mentioned in Suetonius's life of Caligula,* is shown on a relief as a heavy-armed fighter; but he owes his name to the special tactics which he followed as a 'pursuer' of the retiarius. This latter was armed for offence with a net (*rete*), in whose meshes he endeavoured to entangle his opponent, and a trident (*fuscina*); for defence, he wore only the *subligaculum* and *manica*, but this was fixed on the left instead of the right arm, and had attached to it a projecting shoulder-piece (*galeras*), which served to mask the face, in place of a helmet. The net was furnished with a cord (*spira*) by which it could be drawn back if the first cast failed. The *secuior* is sometimes indicated on inscriptions by the symbol > RET. (i.e. *contraretiarius*).

The Thracian (*Thraex*) was introduced by Sulla on his return from the East, when he brought with him a number of prisoners taken in Thrace during the first Mithradatic War. His equipment is partly illustrated by the grave-relief of one M. Antonius Exochus, now lost, but reproduced on Pl. LVII from

* The word *secutorum* has been introduced by some editors into the text of a letter of Cicero (Att. vii. 14. 2) in place of *scutorum*; but Cicero, who here tells us that Caesar had '5,000 shields' at Capua, means by this colloquial term 'heavy-armed fighters'.

a drawing in the Royal Library at Windsor; to the left is seen the short scimitar or *sica*, which he carried in place of a sword; to the right the helmet surmounted by the figure of a griffin, with its perforated vizard turned up. The *balteus, subligaculum*, and *manica* are also shown; and he wears richly decorated greaves (*ocreae*) on *both* legs, and apparently leathern breeches (*fasciae*) as well. He thus had more protective armour than the *hoplomachus*; but this was needful, because he had only a small shield (*parma*), round, square, or even triangular in shape (not shown in the relief). The frequent contests between the *hoplomachus* and the *Thraex* gave rise to the formation of parties in the amphitheatre such as those which grouped themselves about the *factiones* of the circus; and the *parmularius* was a supporter of the 'Thracian' against the bearer of the *scutum*.

Another national type was the *Gallus*. It has been thought that the Gaul was introduced into the arena by Julius Caesar; but Livy quotes a saying of Cato the censor which implies that a 'dying Gaul' might be seen in gladiatorial exhibitions as early as 184 B.C., and it is reasonable to suppose that the Etruscans treated the Celts of Northern Italy in the same manner as the Campanians dealt with their Samnite prisoners. We are expressly told by a good authority that the *Gallus* was afterwards known as the *murmillo*. This is a term derived from the name of a fish, which was represented on the helmet of the *Gallus*; and Festus says that the retiarius, when attacking the *murmillo*, sang the doggerel verse —

Non te peto, piscem peto, quid me fugis, Galle?

The *murmillo* is mentioned several times by Cicero, and seems to have been gradually differentiated from the *Gallus*, since both are mentioned in the same inscription. There is a difficulty with regard to the equipment of the *murmillo*. Ammianus Marcellinus (writing in the fourth century A.D.) compares the Parthian infantry, who were clad in coats of chain-mail, to the *murmillones*; and Tacitus speaks of Gaulish slaves trained to serve as gladiators who wore *continuum ferri tegimen*. These passages would lead us to suppose that the *murmillo* was heavily armed. On the other hand, it is well known that the Gauls disdained defensive armour; and, what is more important, the monuments lend no support to the contrary view. The only relief (now in St. Petersburg) which is declared by its inscription to be that of a *murmillo* represents a gladiator clad in the *subligaculum* only; but there are others on which we see light-armed combatants wearing a tunic, whom there is reason to believe to be *murmillones*. For instance, the relief from Chieti (Pl. LVIII) shows at the left extremity of the frieze two such gladiators, wearing a low helmet, *manica*, and tunic, and carrying a small round shield: they are evidently neither Thracians nor *hoploniachi*, both of which types are clearly depicted in the reliefs, and it is hard to see what name to give them save that of *murmillo*. The round shield must then be the *scutum murmillonicum* of which we read in Festus. The usual adversary of the *murmillo* was the retiarius in the first century A.D., afterwards the *Thraex*.

The types above described were those most commonly engaged in gladiatorial combats: of the rest we know but little. The *provocator*, mentioned by Cicero, is represented on one monument only, and then in Samnite equipment. The *laquearius* differed from the *retiarins* only in the fact that his weapon of offence was the lasso and not the net. The *dimachaerus*, as the name shows, was armed with two cutlasses. The *velites* were called after the light-armed troops of the Roman Republic, and, like them, used the javelin fastened with a thong (*hasta amentata*). Equites, or mounted gladiators, are mentioned in literature, and represented with vizard helmets, small round shields, tunics and guards for arm and thigh; their weapon was a lance. *Essedarii* fought in chariots, after the manner of Gauls and Britons. They are first mentioned in Cicero's letters, and were perhaps introduced into Rome by Julius Caesar, who describes the tactics of the British charioteers (B. G. iv. 33).

SAVAGERY IN SANDALS

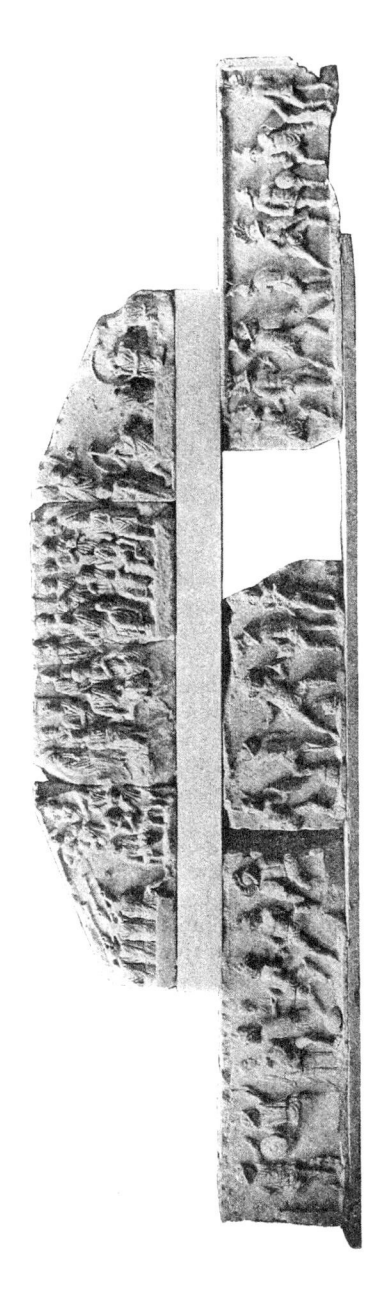

Relief with munus gladiatorium from tomb of C. Lusius Storax
Discovered in Chieti (Teate).

The relief shown on PL LVIII decorated the facade of a tomb at Teate (mod. Chieti), which seems to be identified by an inscription as that of C. Lusius Storax, a freedman who enjoyed the dignity of *sevir Augustalis*, i.e. priest of the Imperial worship, and as such doubtless exhibited the *munus gladiatorium*.* On the slabs which form the pediment we see the *editor muneris* seated in the centre of a group of persons, four of whom—two on either side—occupy *bisellia* and may be identified as the chief magistrates—*quattuorviri iure dicundo*—of the *municipium* of Teate; the two lictors in the background are in attendance on the editor, who enjoyed the privileges of a magistrate on the occasion of the *munus*. At either end of the pediment is a group of musicians—trumpeters (*tubicines*) to left, hornblowers (*cornicines*) to right—whose function it was to rouse the ardour of the gladiators; between the trumpeters and the central group the crowd of excited spectators is represented by four figures whose gesticulations betray the keenness of their interest in the fighting, and these are balanced by a group of attendants engaged in unpacking a box which no doubt contained *missilia*, or presents provided by the editor and scrambled for by the populace. The scene is indicated by a facade of Doric columns, best interpreted as the front of a temple, basilica, or senate-house in the Forum of Teate, which may have been without an amphitheatre when the relief was made. The gladiatorial combats are represented on the slabs of the frieze, of which that in the centre is unfortunately mutilated. For the most part the combatants are to be classed either as 'Samnites' (or *hoplomachi*) or 'Thracians.' Thus on the extreme right we have a group of four fighters, two of whom wear the helmet with feathers, *manica*, *subligaculum* with belt, and leg-guard on the left leg only, and carry the *scutum*, whilst

    * The provision of such spectacles for the public amusement was the most important function of the *seviri*, whose ambition was gratified by the privileges of the *editor muneris*—the wearing of the *praetexta* and the attendance of lictor.

74

the others have guards and *fasciae* on both legs, and small shields (*parmae*). It seems as though the artist, who intends us to regard the first and third as one pair of opponents, the second and fourth as another, may have been clumsily endeavouring to depict a fight between two troops of gladiators (*gregatim pugnantes*). At the other end of the frieze are two figures wearing a low-crowned, broad-brimmed helmet, a tunic and *manica*, but seemingly no leg-guard, and armed with the small round shield. The one on the left, who has dropped his shield and raises his left arm in the direction of the editor, has, we must suppose, been wounded and is demanding the *missio*, which depends on the favour of the spectators;* the other, seen from the back, uplifts his rigid arm in token of victory. We have seen that these are probably *murmillones*. Next to them is seen a Samnite pursuing a Thracian, with two of the attendants (*harenarii*), whose duty it was to remove the dead from the arena, in the background. Then comes a Thracian, whose hands seem to be bound behind his back; unless this be a gesture used in demanding the *missio*, we must take it that he is a criminal condemned to execution. The central figure of the frieze is a Thracian with no helmet, but flowing locks, seen in full face, and probably a portrait.

The relief of Teate is but one among a host of monuments on which gladiators are shown: the tomb of Scaurus, a *duovir* of Pompeii, has a frieze on which is carved the *pompa*, or procession which preceded the show, and in the minor arts (glass and pottery) rude portraits of famous gladiators are amongst

---

* The right of granting the *missio* belonged to the editor, but he usually gratified the wishes of the spectators, who signified their assent by lowering the thumb (*pollicem premere*) or waving a handkerchief (*mappa*), and their refusal of mercy by turning the thumb upward towards the breast (*pollicem vertere, convertere*). Gladiators who had fought bravely were sometimes dismissed without bringing the combat to an issue (*stantes missi*). As a token of final dismissal the gladiator received a wooden sword (*rudis*).

the favourite subjects of decoration. The names of Tetraites and Prudens are specially common; and we read in Petronius of Trimalchio's request that the base of the statue on his tomb should be decorated with 'all the fights of Petraites', which is probably the correct form of the name.

(Jones, 1912)

GRAFFITI

Gladiators Preserved in Time

The ancient Romans, especially the lower orders, including the slaves, were very fond of sketching upon the walls of the ante-rooms (as at Pompeii) such scenes as interested them most; and the greater part of them represent battles of gladiators. These stood in the place of horse-racing, with us; and the people commemorated evidently, and discussed every event of the amphitheatre, as now-a-days they take an interest in what they would have considered, our less-exciting pastime.

These "scratchings" (graffiti), as they are called by Father Garrucci, present to us a class of very rude, but very interesting monuments. One of them records a peculiar occurrence. It is indeed only a battle in the amphitheatre, but it is between two men in very different positions; the names of the combatants are given, as they always are, and numbers over their heads tell you how many victories each one had achieved—in other words, how many public murders he had committed. This battle, then, is between Spiculus, a tyro—that is, one who had never before fought, and Aptonetus, *librarius*, or holding a high office among the gladiators—a man who had gained sixteen victories. The first one has over him the letter V—(*vicit*, he conquered); the other, P—(*periit*, he perished). In fact, the old gladiator, with the sixteen laurels that he had won, is lying on the ground wounded to death, or dead; and the youth who has dared to flesh his sword in that old veteran, is alive, and holding his point towards him, perhaps to dispatch him. Imagine, if you can, the meeting of two such men, without, of course, a particle of moral or noble feeling in their composition; of men who only looked to gaining fame, by the number of murders which they should commit. Imagine the feelings of those two particular men, approaching to meet each other, with the eyes of fifty thousand spectators intent upon them: the one, the old, well experienced fighter, who is indignant at the idea that a stripling like that should have presumed to cope with him, and challenge him to mortal combat; and the other, feeling that if he can carry off those sixteen laurel crowns upon his sword, he will be sung through all Rome, and celebrated, as those men unfortunately were, by public statues and pictures. See them approaching one another; it is a matter of life or death; one must fall; one must die. And in that deep silence of the amphitheatre, when even the breath is bated or suppressed by the spectator, they are drawing near with all the caution of a wild beast, that desires not to be seen or heard by the prey, upon which it is going to spring. Yet each of them has boiling in his breast such a storm of passion as we can hardly imagine. What hatred, in that determined resolve to kill as quick as possible his adversary and rival! What a tumult of wicked murderous passion, yet struggled against, by violent repression, to secure coolness, as necessary in that tremendous crisis, filled those breasts, far beyond our power of conception! No shaking of hands before fighting, as with the skilful contenders in the ring; it is a battle to death, in the presence of the whole city.

Can you not conceive how those hearts throbbed and beat, almost audibly; how those lungs dilated themselves convulsively to breathe, to their full expansion; how both these powerful organs, in their, vital struggles, would almost force out the bony framework of the chest; how the muscles which were thus quickened would twist themselves into knotted cords, and every vessel that fed them would be gorged with a burning stream, and visibly palpitate to the eyes of the entire audience? And by this violent exertion of the nobler organs, and the concurrent intensity of mental determination, would not a corresponding direction, and almost superhuman vigour, be given to the thews and sinews interested in carrying out the brutal instinct (as in mania, or in sudden catastrophes, where powers unknown or dormant are elicited), so as to impart to even secondary parts, sudden and transient development, swelling and tempering them to steel, for only one tremendous moment.

And then, when the swords clash for an instant, and all those evil passions are more thoroughly concentrated, the blow is scarcely seen; one gleam, as of lightning, flashes, when the swords cross, and one falls a corpse to the ground, or may have to receive still his death-blow from the other. It is impossible to imagine deep seated, violent emotions under any other circumstances, that could come near to these, or to study their effects upon the human form equally, under any other circumstances.

(Wiseman, 1863)

School for Gladiators at Pompeii

GLADIATOR SCHOOL

Fight or Die

The gladiators (amongst whom we do not include the condemned criminals—*noxii*—who were sometimes forced to butcher each other in the arena) might be either slaves,* convicts, or free persons (*auctorati*), who were compelled by want to engage themselves in the service of the trainer (*lanista*), from whom the magistrate hired as many pairs (*paria*) as he required for his show.

They were trained on a regular system in barracks or 'schools' (*ludi*), of which the earliest and (up to the close of the Republican period) the most important were at Capua. Such a *ludus* existed at Pompeii in what had at one time been a rectangular *porticus* adjoining the large theatre. All round the colonnade were built cells, sixty-six in number, hardly more than 12 feet square, in two stories with a common kitchen and messroom, and apartments for the *lanista*; and the three entrances were narrow and easily guarded.

Five specimens of gladiatorial armour were discovered in some of the rooms; and in what was evidently a guard-room were found stocks, as well as the skeletons of four prisoners who had been unable to make their escape. In Rome there were several *ludi* established by the emperors; the most important was the *ludus magnus*, near the Colosseum; this is partly represented on fragments of the Marble Plan, which show that in its plan it was similar to that at Pompeii, save for the fact that in the centre of

---

* The humaner legislation of the Antonine period forbade the master of a slave to consign him to the training-school (*ad ludum dare*) without either obtaining his consent or showing good cause.

the court there was an elliptical arena in which the gladiators could practise their art in surroundings resembling those of the amphitheatre.

(Jones, 1912)

Cicero during his consulship speaks of one at Rome, and there were others before his time at Capua and Praeneste. Some of these were set up by wealthy nobles for the purpose of preparing their own gladiators for *mūnera* which they expected to give; others were the property of regular dealers in gladiators, who kept and trained them for hire. The business was almost as disreputable as that of the *lēnōnēs*. During the Empire training-schools were maintained at public expense and under the direction of state officials not only in Rome, where there were four at least of these schools, but also in other cities of Italy where exhibitions were frequently given, and even in the provinces. The purpose of all the schools, public and private alike, was the same, to make the men trained in them as effective fighting machines as possible. The gladiators were in charge of competent training masters (*lanistae*); they were subject to the strictest discipline; their diet was carefully looked after, a special food (*sagīna gladiātōria*) being provided for them; regular gymnastic exercises were prescribed, and lessons given in the use of the various weapons by recognized experts (*magistrī, doctōrēs*). In their fencing bouts wooden swords (*rudēs*) were used. The gladiators associated in a school were collectively called a *familia*.

These schools had also to serve as barracks for the gladiators between engagements, that is, practically as houses of detention. It was from the school of Lentulus at Capua that Spartacus had escaped, and the Romans needed no second lesson of the sort. The general arrangement of these barracks may be understood from the ruins of one uncovered at Pompeii, though in this case the buildings had been originally planned for another purpose, and the rearrangement may not be ideal in all respects.

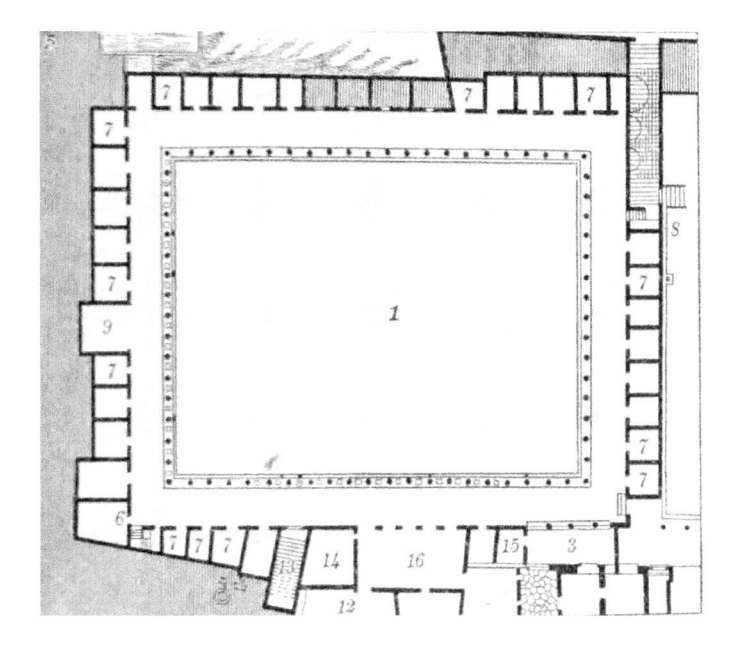

PLAN OF SCHOOL FOR GLADIATORS

A central court, or exercise ground is surrounded by a wide colonnade, and this in turn by rows of buildings two stories in height, the general arrangement being not unlike that of the peristyle of a house. The dimensions of the court are nearly 120 by 150 feet. The buildings are cut up into rooms, nearly all small (about twelve feet square), disconnected and opening upon the court, those in the first story being reached from the colonnade, those in the second from a gallery to which ran several stairways. These small rooms are supposed to be the sleeping-rooms of the gladiators, each accommodating two persons. There are seventy-one of them (marked *7* on the plan), affording room for 142 men. The uses of the larger rooms are purely conjectural. The entrance is supposed to have been at *3*, with a room, *15*, for the watchman or sentinel. At *9* was an *exedra*, where the gladiators may have waited in full panoply for their turns in the exercise ground, *1*. The guard-room, *8*, is identified by the remains of stocks, in which the refractory were fastened for punishment or safe-keeping. They permitted the culprits to lie on their backs or sit in a very uncomfortable position. At *6* was the armory or property room, if we may judge from articles found in it. Near it in the corner was a staircase leading to the gallery before the rooms of the second story. The large room, *16*, was the mess-room, with the kitchen, *12*, opening into it. The stairway, *13*, gives access to the rooms above kitchen and mess-room, possibly the apartments of the trainers and their helpers.

(Johnston, 1903)

From Ancient Sources

GLADIATORS AND WOMEN

Described by Juvenalis and Flaccus

If you marry a wife, it will be that the lyrist Echion or Glaphyrus, or the flute player Ambrosius, may become a father. Then up with a long dais in the narrow street! Adorn your doors and doorposts with wreaths of laurel, that your highborn son, O Lentulus, may exhibit, in his tortoiseshell cradle,* the lineaments of Euryalus (A gladiator) or of a murmillo!†

When Eppia, the senator's wife, ran off with a gladiator‡ to Pharos and the Nile and the ill-famed city of Lagos, Canopus itself cried shame upon the monstrous morals of our town. Forgetful of home, of husband and of sister, without thought of her country, she shamelessly abandoned her weeping children; and—more marvellous still—deserted Paris and the games. Though born in wealth, though as a babe she had slept in a bedizened cradle on the paternal down, she made light of the sea, just as she had long made light of her good name—a loss

---

* The *conopeum* was properly a mosquito-net; here it seems to be used for a bassinette or cradle.

† A *murmillo* was equipped as a Gaulish warrior in heavy armour. He carried the image of a fish in his crest, whence the name μορμύρος or μορμύλος.

‡ *Ludus* is probably a gladiatorial school, or a troop of gladiators.

but little accounted of among our soft litter-riding dames. And so with stout heart she endured the tossing and the roaring of the Tyrrhenian and Ionian Seas, and all the many seas she had to cross. For when danger comes in a right and honourable way, a woman's heart grows chill with fear; she cannot stand upon her trembling feet; but if she be doing a bold, bad thing, her courage fails not. For a husband to order his wife on board ship is cruelty; the bilge-water then sickens her, the heavens go round and round. But if she is running away with a lover, she feels no qualms; then she vomits over her husband; now she messes with the sailors, she roams about the deck, and delights in hauling at the hard ropes.

*****

And what were the youthful charms which captivated Eppia? What did she see in him to allow herself to be called "a she-Gladiator"? Her dear Sergius had already begun to shave; a wounded arm gave promise of a discharge, and there were sundry deformities in his face; a scar caused by the helmet, a huge wen upon his nose, a nasty humour always trickling from his eye. But then he was a gladiator! It is this that transforms these fellows into Hyacinths! it was this that she preferred to children and to country, to sister and to husband. What these women love is the sword; had this same Sergius received his discharge, he would have been no better than a Veiento.*

(Juvenalis and Flaccus, 1918)

---

* Probably the husband.

SAVAGERY IN SANDALS

An Elegy to His Mistress, Complaining that She His Given Preference to a Wealthier Rival. Written by Ovid.

And who now attaches any value to the liberal arts, or looks on poetry as worth a straw? Time was when genius was held more precious than gold; now, if you've no money, you are accounted the veriest barbarian! My books have the good fortune to please my mistress. They have the entrée to her; I, alas, have not. She has given high praise to the poetry, but on the poet she has shut her door. I am told that I'm a genius, yet they leave me to cool my heels where I can. Any rich parvenu who has swash-bucklered his way to wealth is set above me.

Can you, my life, really be so scatter-brained as to put your arms about him? Can you, my life, let him put his arms about you? Let me tell you, in case you know it not, that that head of his was recently covered by a helmet, and that a sword hung from that side which now is so devoted to you. His left hand, with the gold ring which fits it so ill, bore a shield; touch his Tight hand, and you'll find it bathed with blood. The man's a murderer! Can you really hold his hand? What has become of that soft heart of yours? Count those scars, the records of the fights that he's been through. All that he has, he won at the price of his blood. Perhaps he will tell you how many throats he has cut. And are you so greedy for money that you can touch such cruel hands, while I, innocent priest of Apollo and the Muses, vainly lay my verses at your unheeding door?

You, who are wise, learn not our useless poet's lore; learn rather to march with noisy troops and to follow the career of war. Instead of trying to be a poet, learn to be a soldier. Even if you were Homer himself, only thus could you obtain the favours of the fair. Jupiter knew well enough that nothing is so powerful as gold, and he won the virgin on whom be had cast his eye by changing himself to gold.

'He will tell thee how many throats he has cut'

So long as gold was not forthcoming he found himself face to face with an obdurate father, an inflexible damsel, doors of brass and a tower of iron; but no sooner did the would-be seducer arrive with presents than she unveiled her bosom, and forthwith gave—what she was asked to give.

It was not thus in aged Saturn's reign. Then all the metals were buried deep within the bowels of the earth. Bronze and silver, gold and heavy iron to the shades he had committed. In those olden days no treasure heaps were seen. But better things earth gave than that, rich harvests from the unlaborious earth, fruits in abundance and stores of honey laid in the hollow oak. None ever broke the soil with the patient plough, no land surveyor parcelled out the soil; no oars smote the tossing waves. For mortals, then, the shores of the sea were barriers impassable. Against thyself, O Man, hast thou turned thy powers of invention, and used thy genius to invent evils untold. What hath it availed thee to girdle your cities. round with towers and ramparts, and among men to stir up armed war? What is the sea to thee? The earth might have sufficed thee. There is another realm to conquer—the sky; wherefore attack it not? To the heavens, too, thou dost aspire, so far as thou Mayest. Quirinus, Bacchus, Alcides, and, now, Cæsar have each their temple.

We dig the earth for gold instead of golden harvests. The soldier possesses wealth obtained by blood. The Senate shuts its doors against the poor; money paves the way to honours. Money makes the solemn judge, the haughty knight. Let them have everything; let them lord it over the Campus Martius and the Forum; let them decide on peace or war; but in their greediness let them draw the line at robbing me of my mistress, and I shall be content. They must leave something to the poor man.

But nowadays, any woman, be she as prudish as the Sabines, is treated like a chattel-slave by any man who can throw about his money. Now, I'm always stopped by this keeper fellow, and she says that she's in mortal terror of her husband.

If I could afford costly presents, both of them would disappear as by magic. Oh, if there be a god who will avenge the unrequited lover, let him reduce such ill-gotten wealth to dust.

(Naso, 1930)

GLADIATORS AND SUICIDE

Described by Lucilius

For example, there was lately in a training-school for wild-beast gladiators a German, who was making ready for the morning exhibition; he withdrew in order to relieve himself, – the only thing which he was allowed to do in secret and without the presence of a guard. While so engaged, he seized the stick of wood, tipped with a sponge, which was devoted to the vilest uses, and stuffed it, just as it was, down his throat; thus he blocked up his windpipe, and choked the breath from his body. That was truly to insult death!

Yes, indeed; it was not a very elegant or becoming way to die; but what is more foolish than to be over-nice about dying? What a brave fellow! He surely deserved to be allowed to choose his fate! How bravely he would have wielded a sword! With what courage he would have hurled himself into the depths of the sea, or down a precipice! Cut off from resources on every hand, he yet found a way to furnish himself with death, and with a weapon for death. Hence you can understand that nothing but the will need postpone death. Let each man judge the deed of this most zealous fellow as he likes, provided we agree on this point, – that the foulest death is preferable to the fairest slavery.

Inasmuch as I began with an illustration taken from humble life, I shall keep on with that sort. For men will make greater demands upon themselves, if they see that death can be despised even by the most despised class of men. The Catos, the Scipios, and the others whose names we are wont to hear with admiration, we regard as beyond the sphere of imitation; but I shall now prove to you that the virtue of which I speak is found as frequently in the gladiators' training-school as among the leaders in a civil war.

Lately a gladiator, who had been sent forth to the morning exhibition, was being conveyed in a cart along with the other prisoners; nodding as if he were heavy with sleep, he let his head fall over so far that it was caught in the spokes; then he kept his body in position long enough to break his neck by the revolution of the wheel. So he made his escape by means of the very wagon which was carrying him to his punishment.

When a man desires to burst forth and take his departure, nothing stands in his way. It is an open space in which Nature guards us. When our plight is such as to permit it, we may look about us for an easy exit. If you have many opportunities ready to hand, by means of which you may liberate yourself, you may make a selection and think over the best way of gaining freedom; but if a chance is hard to find, instead of the best, snatch the next best, even though it be something unheard of, something new. If you do not lack the courage, you will not lack the cleverness, to die.

See how even the lowest class of slave, when suffering goads him on, is aroused and discovers a way to deceive even the most watchful guards! He is truly great who not only has given himself the order to die, but has also found the means. I have promised you, however, some more illustrations drawn from the same games.

During the second event in a sham sea-fight one of the barbarians sank deep into his own throat a spear which had been given him for use against his foe. "Why, oh why," he said, "have I not long ago escaped from all this torture and all this mockery? Why should I be armed and yet wait for death to come?" This exhibition was all the more striking because of the lesson men learn from it that dying is more honourable than killing.

(Seneca, 1917)

Famous Gladiators

A List of Gladiators

Mentioned in History

COLUMBUS, a mirmillo in the time of Caligula, was vanquished by Thrax and afterwards, when recovering, had his wound poisoned by the emperor.

COLUMBUS, another gladiator, lived under Nero.

COLUMBUS was also the name of a gladiator overcome by SPICULUS.

PROCULUS, lived also in the favor of Caligula, but was later executed by him. His name occurs in the gladiatorial armory of Pompeii.

SPICULUS, lived in the time of Nero, became a favorite of the emperor; later executed by GALBA. The name occurs on the walls of Pompeii.

TETRAITES, vanquisher of PRUDES, was represented on the beaker of Trimalchius.

PRUDES or PRUDENS, was a gladiator vanquished by TRETRAITES.

HERMES, is mentioned on the walls of Pompeii, lived in time of Nero.

HERMAS, another gladiator is mentioned many times by Martial.

CRESCENS, lived in the beginning of the 2nd century A.D.

PETRAITES, is assumed, but with question, to be identical with TETRAITES.

MEROPS, HERMES, PRUDES and COLUMBUS were vanquished by GAMUS, CALAMIS, TETRAITES and SPICULUS.

Of the less famous champions the names IERAX, OLYMPIE, ANTILOCE, CRESCENS, PYRAMUS, HOLES, CUCUMBUS and AEMILIUS are mentioned.

(Eisen, 1927)

SPARTACUS

A Collection of Writings

Spartacus was a Thracian by birth, and had been compelled, like other barbarians, to serve in the Roman army, from which he had deserted, and, at the head of a body of chosen companions, had carried on a partisan war against the conquerors. Being made prisoner, Spartacus was sold as a slave; and his strength and size caused him to be reserved as a gladiator. He was placed in a gladiatorial school at Capua, with two hundred other Thracian, German and Gaulish slaves, among whom a conspiracy was formed for effecting their escape. Their plot was discovered; but a small body, under Spartacus, broke out, and, having procured arms, and gained some advantages over the Roman forces sent against them, they were soon joined by the slaves and peasantry of the neighbourhood, and their numbers amounted to 10,000 men. By the courage and skill of Spartacus, several considerable battles were gained; but his authority was insufficient to restrain the ferocity and licentiousness of his followers, and the cities of the south of Italy were pillaged with the most revolting atrocities. In a few months, Spartacus found himself at the head of 60,000 men; and the consuls were now sent, with two legions, against the revolted slaves. Mutual jealousies divided the leaders of the latter, and the Gauls and Germans formed a separate body under their own leaders, while the Thracians and Lucanians adhered to Spartacus. The former were defeated; but Spartacus skilfully covered their retreat, and successively defeated the two consuls. Flushed with success, his followers demanded to be led against Rome; and the city trembled before the servile forces. In this crisis, Licinius Crassus, who was afterwards a triumvir, was placed at the head of the army. His lieutenant, Mummius, whom he dispatched with two legions to watch the motions of the enemy, was defeated by a superior force, and slain. Crassus, after having made an example of the defeated legions, by executing every tenth man, surrounded Spartacus, near Rhegium, with a ditch six miles in length. Spartacus broke through the enemy by night; but Crassus, who did not doubt that he would march upon Rome, pursued him, and defeated a considerable part of his forces, who had abandoned their general from disaffection. Spartacus now retreated; but his followers compelled him to lead them against the Romans. His soldiers fought with a courage deserving success; but they were overcome, after an obstinate conflict, and Spartacus himself fell fighting on his knees, upon a heap of his slain enemies. According to the Soman statements, 60,000 rebels fell in this battle, 6000 were made prisoners, and crucified on the Appian way. A considerable number escaped, and continued the war, but were finally destroyed by Pompey.

(Blake, 1861)

The Revolt of the Gladiators

At the beginning of the first Punic War, or war with Carthage, a new form of entertainment was introduced into Rome. This was the gladiatorial show, the fights of armed men in the arena, the first of which was given in the year 264 B.C., at the funeral of D. Junius Brutus. These exhibitions were long confined to funeral occasions, money being frequently left for this purpose in wills, but they gradually extended to other occasions, and finally became the choice amusement of the brutal Roman mob. The gladiators were divided into several classes, in accordance with their particular weapons and modes of fighting, and great pains were taken to instruct them in the use of their special arms. But in the period that followed the death of Sulla Rome was to have a gladiatorial exhibition of a different sort.

In the city of Capua was a school of gladiators, kept by a man named Lentulus. It was his practice to hire out his trained pupils to nobles for battles in the arena during public festivals. His school was a large one, and included in its numbers a Thracian named Spartacus, who had been taken prisoner while leading his countrymen against the Romans, and was to be punished for his presumption by making sport for his conquerors.

But Spartacus had other and nobler aims. He formed a plot of flight to freedom in which two hundred of his fellows joined, though only seventy-eight succeeded in making their escape. These men, armed merely with the knives and spits which they had seized as they fled, made their way to the neighbouring mountains, and sought a refuge in the crater of Mount Vesuvius. It must be borne in mind that this mountain, in that year of 73 B.C., was silent and seemingly extinct, though before another century passed it was to awake to vital activity. It was only biding its time in slumber.

It was better to die on the open field than in the amphitheatre, argued Spartacus, and his followers agreed with him. Their position in the crater was a strong one, and the news of their revolt soon brought them a multitude of allies,—slaves and outlaws of every kind. These Spartacus organized and drilled, supplying them with officers from the gladiators, mostly old soldiers, and placing them under rigid discipline. It was liberty he wanted, not rapine, and he did his utmost to restrain his lawless followers from acts of violence.

Pompey, the chief Roman general of that day, was then absent in Spain, fighting with a remnant of the Marian forces. Two Roman prætors led their forces against the gladiators, but were driven back with loss, and the army of Spartacus swelled day by day. The wild herdsmen of Apulia joined him in large numbers. They were slaves to their lords, whom they hated bitterly, and here was an opening for freedom and revenge.

It was soon evident that Rome had on its hands the greatest and most dangerous of its servile wars. Spartacus was brave and prudent, and possessed the qualities of an able leader.

Unfortunately for him, he led an unmanageable host. In the next year both the consuls took the field against him. By this time his army had swelled to more than one hundred thousand men, and with these he pushed his way northward through the passes of the Apennines. But now insubordination appeared. Crixus, one of his lieutenants, ambitious of independent command, led off a large division of the army, chiefly Germans. He was quickly punished for his temerity, being surprised and slain with the whole of his force.

Spartacus, wise enough to know that he could not long hold out against the whole power of Rome, kept on northward, hoping to pass the Alps and find a place of refuge remote from the stronghold of his foes. Both the consuls attacked him in his march, and both were defeated, while he retaliated on Rome by forcing his prisoners to fight as gladiators in memory of the slain Crixus.

Reaching the provinces of the north, his diminished force was repulsed by Crassus, one of the richest men of Rome, who had taken the field as prætor. Spartacus would still have fought his way towards the Alps but for his followers, whose impatient thirst for rapine forced him to march southward again.

Every Roman force that assailed him on this march was hurled back in defeat. He even meditated an attack on Rome itself, but relinquished this plan as too desperate, and instead employed his men in collecting arms and treasure from the cities of central and southern Italy. Discipline was almost at an end. The wild horde of slaves and outlaws were beyond any strict military control. So great and general were their ravages that in a later day the poet Horace promised his friend a jar of wine made in the Social War, "if he could find one that had escaped the ravages of roaming Spartacus."

In the year 71 B.C. the most vigorous efforts were made to put down this dangerous revolt. Pompey was still in Spain. The only man at home of any military reputation was the prætor Crassus, who had amassed an enormous fortune by buying up property at famine prices during the Proscription of Sulla, and in speculative measures since.

He was given full command, took the field with a large army, restored discipline to the beaten bands of the consuls by cruel and rigorous measures, and assailed Spartacus in Calabria, where he was seeking to rekindle the Servile War, or slave outbreak, in Sicily. He had even engaged with pirate captains to transport a part of his force to Sicily, but the freebooters took the money and sailed away without the men.

And now began a struggle for life and death. Spartacus was in the narrowest part of the foot of Southern Italy. Crassus determined to keep him there by building strong lines of intrenchment across the neck of land. Spartacus attacked his works twice in one day, but each time was repulsed with great slaughter. But he defended himself vigorously.

Pompey was now returning from Spain. Crassus, not caring to be robbed of the results of his labours, determined to assault Spartacus in his camp. But before he could do so the daring gladiator attacked his lines again, forced his way through, and marched for Brundusium, where he hoped to find ships that would convey him and his men from Italy.

As it happened, a large body of Roman veterans, returning from Macedonia, had just reached Brundusium, and undertook its defence. Foiled in his purpose, Spartacus turned upon the pursuing army of Crassus, like a wolf at bay, and attacked it with the energy of desperation. The battle that ensued was contested with the fiercest courage. Spartacus and his men were fighting for their lives, and the result continued doubtful till the brave gladiator was wounded in the thigh by a javelin. Falling on his knee, he fought with the courage of a hero until, overpowered by numbers, he fell dead.

His death decided the conflict. Most of his followers were slain on the field. A strong body escaped to the mountains, but these were pursued, and many fell. Five thousand of them made their way to the north of Italy, where they were met by Pompey, on his return from Spain, and slaughtered to a man.

Crassus took six thousand prisoners, and these he disposed of in the cruel Roman way of dealing with revolted slaves, hanging or crucifying the whole of them along the road between Rome and Capua.

Thus ended far the most important outbreak of Roman gladiators and slaves. The south of Italy suffered horribly from its ravages, but not through any act of Spartacus, who throughout showed a moderation equal to his courage and military ability. Had it not been for the lawless character of his followers his career might have had a very different ending, for he had shown himself a commander of rare ability and unconquerable courage.

(Morris, 1896)

Spartacus, Crixus, and the Revolt

The Romans had many virtues, and conspicuous amongst these was the virtue of impartiality. They treated everybody with equal inhumanity. They were as pitiless towards the humble as towards the proud. The quality of mercy was utterly unknown to them. Their motto,

"Parcere subjectis, et debellare superbos,"

Powell Buxton has happily translated, "They murdered all who resisted them, and enslaved the rest."
(…)
We speak of Spartacus, who defeated many Roman armies, and disputed with the all-conquering republic the dominion of the Italian Peninsula, and with it that of the civilized world. This war took place B.C. 73-71, while Rome was engaged in hostilities with Sertorius and Mithridates; and it was brought to an end only by the exertions of the ablest generals the republic then had,—the great Pompeius having been summoned from Spain,

and it being in contemplation to order home Lucullus from the East. In the war with Hannibal the Romans showed their fearlessness by sending troops to Spain while the Carthaginian with his army was lying under their walls; but they called troops and generals from Spain to their assistance against the Thracian gladiator. He must have been a man of extraordinary powers to have accomplished so much with the means at his disposal. It has been regarded as a proof of the astonishing powers of Hannibal as a commander, that he could keep together, and in effective condition, an army composed of the outcasts, as it were, of many nations, and win with it great victories, scattered over a long period of time; yet this was less than was done by Spartacus. The Carthaginian, like Alexander, succeeded to an army formed by his father, next after himself the ablest man of the age. The Thracian, without country or home, and an outlaw from the beginning of his enterprise, had to create an army, and that out of the most heterogeneous and apparently the most unpromising materials. The palm must be aligned to the latter.

To what race did Spartacus belong? We are told that he was a Thracian, his family being shepherds. Plutarch pays him the highest compliment in his power, by admitting that he deserved to be regarded as belonging to the Hellenic race. He was, says the old Lifemaker, "a man not only of great courage and strength, but, in judgment and mildness of character, superior to his condition, and more like a Greek than one would expect from his nation." It is not impossible that he had Greek blood in his veins. Thrace was hard by Greece, had many Greek cities, and its full proportion of those Greek adventurers, military and civil, who were to be found in every country and city, from Spain to Persia, from Gades to Ecbatana. What more probable than that among his ancestors were Greeks? At the same time it must be admitted that the Thracians themselves were capable of producing eminent men, being a superior physical race, and prevented only by the force of circumstances from attaining to a respectable position. They were renowned for soldierlike qualities, which caused the

Romans to give them the preference as gladiators,—a dubious honor, to say the best of it.

How, and under what circumstances, Spartacus became a gladiator, is a point by no means clear. We cannot trust the Roman accounts, as it was a meritorious thing, in the opinion of a Roman, for a man to lie for his country, as well as to die for it. Florus states, that he was first a Thracian mercenary, then a Roman soldier, then a deserter and robber, and then, because of his strength, a gladiator from choice. But, to say nothing of the national prejudices of Florus, he writes like a man who felt it to be a particular grievance that Romans should have been compelled to fight slaves, and particularly gladiators. This is in striking contrast with Plutarch, who was a contemporary of Florus, but whose patriotic pride was not wounded by the victories which the Thracian gladiator won over Roman generals. Indeed, as he was willing to admit that Spartacus ought to have been a Greek, we may suppose that he was pleased to read of his victories,—a not unnatural thing in a provincial, and particularly in a Greek, who knew so well what his country had once been. Plutarch says not a word about the Thracian having been a soldier and a thief, but introduces him with one of his good stories. "They say," he tells us, "that when Spartacus was first taken to Rome to be sold, a snake was seen folded over his face while he was sleeping, and a woman, of the same tribe with Spartacus, who was skilled in divination, and possessed by the mysterious rites of Dionysus, declared that this was a sign of a great and formidable power, which would attend him to a happy termination." She was the Thracian's wife, or mistress, being connected with him by some tender tie, and was with him when he subsequently escaped from Capua. In the bloody drama of the War of Spartacus hers is the sole relieving figure, and we would fain know more of her, for it could have been no ordinary woman who was loved by such a man.

The passion of the Romans for gladiatorial combats is well known. Not a few persons followed the calling of gladiator-trainers, and had whole corps of these doomed men, whom they let to those who wished to get up such shows. There were several schools of gladiators, the chief of which were at Ravenna and Capua, where garrisons were maintained to keep the pupils in subjection. According to one account, Spartacus, while on a predatory incursion, was made prisoner, and afterwards sold to Cneius Lentulus Batiatus, a trainer of gladiators, who sent him to his school at Capua. He was to have fought at Rome. But he had higher thoughts than of submitting to so degrading a destiny as the being "butchered to make a Roman holiday." Most of his companions were Gauls and Thracians, the bravest of men, who bore confinement with small patience. They conspired to make their escape,—the chief conspirators being Spartacus and two others, who were subsequently made his lieutenants,—Crixus, a Gaul, and Œnomaus, a Greek. Some two hundred persons were in the conspiracy, but only a portion of them succeeded in breaking the school bounds. Florus says that not more than thirty got out, while Velleius makes the number to have been sixty-four, and Plutarch seventy-eight. Having armed themselves with spits, knives, and cleavers, from a cook's shop, they hastened out of Capua. Passing along the Appian Way, they fell in with a number of wagons loaded with gladiators' weapons, which they seized, and were thus placed in good fighting condition. Shortly after this they encountered a small body of soldiers, whom they routed, and whose arms they substituted for the gladiatorial, deeming these no longer worthy of them.

They were now joined by a few others, fugitives and mountaineers, with whom they took refuge in the crater of Vesuvius, then, as from time immemorial, and for nearly a century and a half later, inactive. Thence, under the leadership of Spartacus and his lieutenants, Crixus and Œdomaus, they ravaged the country; but it is not probable that they caused much alarm, their number being only two hundred, and such collections of slaves being by no means uncommon. The Romans little dreamed that they were on the eve of one of the most terrible of their many wars. Claudius Pulcher, one of the Prætors, was sent against the "robbers," as they were considered to be. He found them so advantageously posted on the mountain, that, though superior to them in numbers in the ratio of fifteen to one, he resolved to blockade them, and so compel them to descend to the plain and fight at disadvantage, or starve. But he was contending with a man of genius, against whom even Rome's military system could not then succeed. He despised his enemy,—a sort of gratification which to those indulging in it generally costs very dear. Spartacus caused ropes to be made of vine branches, with the aid of which he and his followers lowered themselves to the base of the mountain, at a point which had been left unguarded by the Romans because considered inaccessible by the red-tapist who commanded them, and consequently affording a capital outlet for bold men under a daring leader. In the dead of night the gladiators stole round to the rear of the Roman camp, and assailed it. Taken by surprise and heavy with sleep, the Romans were routed like sheep, and their arms and baggage passed into the hands of the despised enemy.

Spartacus saw now that it was time for him and his comrades to assume a higher character than had hitherto belonged to them. Instead of a leader of outlaws, he aspired to be the liberator of the servile population of Italy. He issued a proclamation, in which, while calling upon his followers to remember the multitudes who groaned in chains, he urged the slaves to rise, pointing out how strong they were and how weak were their oppressors, maintaining that the strength of the masters lay in the blind and disgraceful submission of the slaves, at the same time declaring that the land belonged of right to the bravest,—a sentiment as natural and proper when uttered by a man in his situation as it is base when proceeding from a modern buccaneer, who has taken up arms, not to obtain his own freedom, but to enslave others. The whole address is contemptuous towards the Romans, though somewhat too rhetorical for a man in the situation of Spartacus. It is the composition of Sallust, but we may believe that it expresses the sentiments of Spartacus, as Sallust was not only his contemporary, but was too good an artist to disregard keeping in what he wrote.

The country being full of slaves and the children of slaves, Spartacus had little difficulty in obtaining recruits. Apulia was particularly fruitful of insurgents. In that country the vices of Roman slavery were displayed in all their naked hideousness, and the Apulian shepherds and herdsmen had a reputation for lawlessness that has never been surpassed. From assailing travellers, the marauders began to plunder the smaller country-houses; and all but the rich were obliged to desert the country, and flock into the towns. So early as the year 185 B.C., seven thousand slaves in Apulia were condemned for brigandage by a Praetor sent specially to restore order in that land of pasturage. When they were not employed upon the hills, they were shut up in large, prison-like buildings, (*ergastula*) where they talked over their wrongs, and formed schemes of vengeance." The century and more between this date and the appearance of Spartacus had not improved the condition of the Apulian slaves. He found them ripe for revolt, and was soon joined by thousands of their number, men whose modes of life rendered them the very best possible material for soldiers, provided they could be induced to submit to the restraints of discipline. They were strong, hardy, athletic, and active, and full of hatred of their masters. It shows the superiority of the Thracian that he could prevail upon them to act in a regular manner. He formed them into an army, the chief officers being the men who had escaped from Capua in his company. This army had some discipline, which was the more easily acquired because many of the men were originally soldiers, captives of the Roman sword. But the hatred of all in it to the Romans, and their knowledge that they had to choose between victory and the crudest forms of death known to the crudest of conquerors, made them the most reliable military force then to be found in the world.

With such an army, thus composed, thus animated, and thus

led, Spartacus commenced that war to which he has given his name. Bursting upon Lower Italy, the most horrible atrocities were perpetrated, the rich landholders being subjected to every species of indignity and cruelty, in accordance with that law of retaliation which was accepted and recognized by all the ancient world, and which the modern has not entirely abrogated. Towns were captured and destroyed, and the slaves everywhere liberated to swell the conquering force. Spartacus is said to have sought to moderate the fury of his followers, and we can believe that he did so without supposing that he was much above his age in humane sentiment. He saw that excesses were likely to demoralize his army, and so render it unfit to meet the legions which it must sooner or later encounter.

Much as Spartacus had done, and signal as had been his successes, it was not yet the opinion at Rome that he was a formidable foe. The government despatched Publius Varinius Glaber to act against him, at the head of ten thousand men. This seems a small force, yet it was not much smaller than the army with which, three or four years later, Lucullus overthrew the whole military power of the Armenian monarchy; and it was half as large as that with which Cæsar changed the fate of the world at Pharsalia. The Romans probably thought it strong enough to subdue all the slaves in Italy, and Varinius sufficiently skilful to defeat their leaders and send them to Rome in chains. But they were to have a rough awakening from their dreams of invincibility, though some early successes of Varinius for a time apparently justified their confidence.

The army of Spartacus numbered forty thousand men, but it was poorly armed, and its discipline was very imperfect. It still lacked, to use a modern term, "the baptism of fire,"—never yet having been matched in the open field against a regular force. Its arms were chiefly agricultural implements, and wooden pikes that had been made by hardening the points of stakes with fire. Spartacus resolved upon retreating into Lucania; but the Gauls in his army, headed by his lieutenant Crixus, pronounced this decision cowardly, separated themselves from the main body, attacked the Romans, and were utterly routed. The retreat to Lucania was then made in perfect safety, and even with glory, apart from the skill with which it was conducted. Watching his opportunity, and showing that he understood the military principle of cutting up an enemy in detail, Spartacus fell upon a Roman detachment, two thousand strong, and destroyed it. Shortly after this, the Roman general succeeded, as he thought, in getting him into a trap. The servile encampment was upon a piece of ground hemmed in on one side by mountains, on the other by impassable waters, and the Romans were about to close up the only outlets with some of those grand works to which they owed so many of their conquests, when, one night, Spartacus silently retreated, leaving his camp in such a state as completely deceived the enemy, who did not discover what had happened until the next morning, when the gladiators were beyond their reach.

This masterly retreat was followed up by a brilliant surprise of a division of the Roman army under the command of Cossinius. The night was just getting in, and the soldiers were resting from their day's march and from the labors of forming the encampment, when the Thracian fell upon them. Thus suddenly attacked, they fled, without making any show of resistance,— abandoning everything to the assailants. Cossinius himself, who was bathing, had time only to escape with his life. The Romans rallied, a battle ensued, and they were routed, Cossinius being among the slain. This action took place not far from the Aufidus, which had witnessed the slaughter of Cannæ.

Spartacus now considered his army fairly "blooded." It had routed a Roman detachment, and defeated a small army. Two Roman camps had fallen into its hands, under circumstances that gave indications of superior generalship, and several towns had been stormed. Though still deficient in arms, he resolved to attack Varinius. Sallust represents him as addressing his army before the battle, and telling them that they were about to enter, not upon a single action, but upon a long war,—that from success, then, would follow a series of victories,—and that therein lay their only salvation from a death at once excruciating and infamous. They must, he said, live upon victory after victory,— an expression that showed he had a clear comprehension of the nature of his situation. In the battle that followed, Varinius was beaten, unhorsed, and compelled to fly for his life. All his personal goods fell into the hands of Spartacus. His lictors, with the *fasces*, shared the same fate. Spartacus assumed the dress of the Roman, and all the ensigns of authority. He has been censured for this; but a little reflection ought to convince every one that he did not act from vanity, but from a profound appreciation of the state of things in Italy. The slaves, of which his army was composed, were accustomed to see the emblems of authority with which he was now clothed and surrounded in the possession of their masters alone; and when they beheld them on and about their chief, they were not only reminded of the governing power, but also of the overthrow of those who had therefore monopolized it. Spartacus was a statesman; and knew how to operate on the minds of the rude masses who followed him and obeyed his orders.

The defeat of Varinius left the whole of Lower Lucania at the mercy of the gladiators. Spartacus now established posts at Metapontum and at Thurii. Here he laboured, with unceasing energy and industry, to organize and discipline his men. Adopting various measures to prevent them from becoming enervated through the abundance in which they were revelling, he prohibited the use of money among them, and gave all that he himself had to relieve those who had suffered from the war. Some of his officers are said to have followed his example in making so great a sacrifice for the common good.

Towards the close of the year Varinius had succeeded in getting another army on foot. With this he resolved to watch the enemy,—repeated defeats having made the Romans cautious, though they were not even yet seriously alarmed. He formed and fortified a camp, whence he kept a look-out. There was some skirmishing, but no fighting on a large scale. This did not suit Spartacus, who had become confident in himself and his men. He desired battle, but wished the Romans should take the initiative, and was convinced that the near approach of winter would compel them soon to fight or to retreat. To encourage them, he feigned fear, and commenced a retrograde movement; but no sooner had the elated Romans advanced in pursuit than he turned upon them, and they were compelled to fight under circumstances that made defeat certain. This second rout of Varinius was total, and we hear no more of him.

Never had there been a more successful campaign than that which Spartacus had just closed. His force had been increased from less than one hundred men to nearly one hundred thousand. He had proved himself more than the equal of the generals who had been sent against him, both in strategy and in arms. He had fought three great battles, and numerous lesser actions, and had been uniformly successful. Like Carnot, he had "organized victory." A large part of Italy was at his command, and, under any other circumstances than those which existed, or against any other foe than Rome, he would probably have found little difficulty in establishing a powerful state, the origin of which would have been far more respectable than of that with which he was contending. But he was a statesman, and knew, that, brilliant as were his successes, he had no chance of accomplishing anything permanent within the Peninsula. He was fighting, too, for freedom, not for dominion. His plan was to get out of Italy. Two courses were open to him. He might retreat to the extremity of the Peninsula, cross the strait that separates it from Sicily, and renew the servile wars of that island; or he might march north, force his way out of Italy, and so with most of his followers reach their homes in Gaul and Thrace. The latter course was determined upon; but the more hot-headed portion of his men, the Gauls, were opposed to it, and resolved to march upon Rome. A division of the victorious army ensued. The larger number, under Spartacus, proceeded to carry out the wise plan of their leader, but the minority refused to obey him. We have seen, that, at the very outset of his enterprise, Spartacus encountered opposition from the Gauls in his army, who were ever for rash measures, and that, separating themselves from their associates, under the lead of Crixus, they had been defeated. Crixus rejoined his old chieftain, and did good service; but he and his countrymen, untaught by experience, and inflated with a notion of invincibility,—on what founded, it would be hard to say,—would not aid Spartacus in his prudent attempt to lead his followers out of Italy. Rome was their object, and, to the number of thirty thousand, they separated themselves from the main army. At first, the event seemed to justify their decision. Meeting a Roman army, commanded by the Prætor Arrius, on the borders of Samnium, the Gauls put it to rout, and the victory of Crixus was not less decisive than any of those which had been won by Spartacus. But this splendid dawn was soon overcast. Crixus was a drunkard, and, while sleeping off one of his fits of intoxication, he was set upon by a Roman army under the Consul Gellius. He was killed, and his followers either shared his fate or were totally dispersed. This was the first great victory won by the Romans in the war.

The defeat of Varinius aroused the Roman government to see that their enemy was not to be despised, and, revolted slave though he was, they were compelled to pay him the respect of making prodigious efforts to effect his destruction. The Consuls Gellius and Lentulus were charged with the conduct of the war. The former overthrew the Gauls. The latter followed Spartacus, and came up with him in Etruria. Here a contest of pure generalship took place. Lentulus was determined not to fight until Gellius—whose victory he knew of—should have come up; and Spartacus was equally determined that fight he should before the junction could be effected. He succeeded in blocking up the road by which Gellius was advancing, unknown to Lentulus, and then offered the latter battle. Supposing that his colleague would join him in the course of the action, the Roman accepted the challenge and was beaten. The victors then marched to meet Gellius, who was served after the same manner as Lentulus. Spartacus was the only general who ever defeated two great Roman armies, each headed by a Consul, on the same day, and in different battles. Hannibal's Austerlitz, Cannæ, approaches nearest to this exploit of the Thracian; but on that field the two consular armies were united under the command of Varro.

These great successes were soon followed by the defeat of two lesser Roman armies, combined under the lead of the Prætor Manlius and the Proconsul Cassius. This last victory not only left the whole open country at the command of Spartacus, but also the road to Rome, upon which city he now resolved to march. It would have been wiser, had he persevered in his original plan, the execution of which his victories must have made it easy to carry out. But perhaps success had its usual effect, even on his mind, and blinded him to the impossibility of permanent triumph in Italy. He winnowed his army, dismissing all his soldiers except such as were distinguished by their bravery, their strength, and their intelligence. In order that his march might be swift, he caused all the superfluous baggage to be destroyed. Every beast of burden that could be dispensed with was slain. His prisoners were disposed of after the same fashion. In a modern general such an act would be utterly without excuse. But it was strictly in accordance with the laws of ancient warfare, and Spartacus probably felt far more regret at sacrificing his beasts of burden than he experienced in consenting to, if he did not order, the butchery of some thousands of men whom he must have looked upon as so many brutes.

Proceeding to the south, Spartacus fell in with a great Roman army led by Arrius, and a battle was fought near Ancona, in which victory was true to the gladiator. The Romans were not only beaten, their army was utterly destroyed; a result which they seem to have felt to be so shameful, that they made no apologies for it. Why, after this signal victory, Spartacus did not forthwith carry out his grand design of attacking Rome,—a design every way so worthy of his genius, and which alone could give him a chance of achieving permanent success after he had abandoned the idea of forcing his way out of Italy by a northern march,—can never be known. It is supposed to have been in consequence of information that circumstances had now placed it in his power to effect a passage into Sicily, a project which he had regarded with favor at an earlier period.

At this time the Cilician pirates had the command of the Mediterranean, which they held until they were conquered, some years later, by Pompeius. It was by the aid of these men that Spartacus expected to carry his army into Sicily. They had shipping in abundance, and in a few days they could have conveyed a hundred thousand men across the narrow strait that separates Sicily from Italy. This they agreed to do, and were paid in advance by Spartacus, though it is probable that he relied less upon that payment for their assistance than upon the palpable fact that their interests were the same as his own. The pirates were on the sea what the gladiatorial army was on land. They were the victims of Roman oppression, and had become outlaws because the world's law was against them. A union of their fleets, which numbered more than a thousand vessels, with the army of Spartacus, in the harbors and on the fields of Sicily, would perhaps have been more than a match for the whole power of Rome, contending as the republic then was with Mithridates, and bleeding still from the wounds inflicted by Marius and Sulla, as well as from the blows of Spartacus. Sicily, too, was then in a state which promised well for the design of the Thracian. Verres was ruling over the island,—and how he ruled it Cicero has told us. Had the victorious Thracian entered the island, both the free population and the slaves would have risen against the Romans. A new state might have been formed, strong both in fleets and in armies, and compelled from the very nature of its origin to contend to the death with its old oppressors. Whatever the result, it is certain that a long Sicilian war, like that which the Romans had been compelled to wage with the Carthaginians, would have changed the course of history, by directing the attention and the energies of such men as Crassus, Pompeius, and Cæsar to very different fields from those on which their fame and power were won.

But it was not to be. There was work for Rome to do, which could be done by no other nation. The power that had been found superior to Hannibal was not to fall before Spartacus, or even to have its course stayed materially by his victories. He marched to the foot of Italy, on the shore of the strait, where he expected to find his supposed naval allies. He was disappointed. They, impolitic no less than faithless, broke their engagement after they had pocketed the sum agreed upon for their services. It was impossible for Spartacus to carry out his design; for not only had he no vessels, but his followers were, it is altogether probable, incapable of building them. The Romans, too, must have had ships in the strait, and a very few would have been found enough to keep it clear of the unskilful gladiators, even had the latter had the time and the means to construct boats.

After the defeat of the Romans under Arrius, the Senate had called Crassus to the chief command, resolving to make an herculean effort to destroy their terrible enemy. The accounts are somewhat confused, but, according to Plutarch, Crassus commenced operations against Spartacus before the latter marched for Sicily. He sent one of his lieutenants, Mummius, to follow and harass the gladiators, but with orders to avoid a general engagement. The lieutenant disobeyed his orders, fought a battle, and was defeated. Not a few of his men threw away their arms, and fled,—an uncommon thing with a Roman army. The victors continued their march, but, as we have seen, failed in their main object. Spartacus then took up a position in the territory of Rhegium, which is over against Sicily. He must have been convinced by this time that the crisis of his fortune had arrived, and though he would not even then entirely give up all idea of crossing over into the island that lay within sight of his camp, he prepared to meet the coming storm, which had been for some time gathering in his rear. Accordingly he faced about, and commenced a game of generalship with Crassus, who was now in person at the head of the Roman army.

Of all men then living, Crassus was best entitled to command an army employed in fighting revolted slaves. If not the greatest slaveholder in Rome, he was the most systematic of the class of owners, and knew best how to turn the industry of slaves to account. He was the wealthiest citizen of the republic. One can understand how indignant such a person must have felt at the audacity of the gladiator and his followers. As a slaveholder, as a man of property, as a lover of law and order, he was concerned at so very disorderly a spectacle as that of slaves subverting all the laws of the republic; as a Roman, he felt that abhorrence for slaves which was common to the character. Here were motives enough to bring out the powers of any man, if powers he had in him; and it does not follow that because Crassus was very rich he was therefore a fool. He was a man of consummate talents, and at this particular time was probably the most influential citizen of Rome. The Romans had confidence in him, as the embodiment of the spirit of supremacy by which they were so completely animated. The event showed that their confidence was not misplaced.

The army of Crassus was two hundred thousand strong, and having restored its discipline by examples of great severity, he marched to meet Spartacus; but on arriving in front of the latter's position, he would not attack it, while Spartacus showed an equal unwillingness to fight. The Roman determined to blockade the enemy. As they had the sea on one side, and that was held by a fleet, he commenced a line of works, the completion of which would have rendered it impossible for the gladiators to escape. These works were on the usual Roman scale, and consisted principally of walls and ditches, a hundred thousand men being employed in their construction. So cleverly did Crassus conceal what he was about, that it was not until he had almost accomplished his design that Spartacus discovered the intention of his foe. The emergency was suited to his genius, and he was not unequal to it. He began a series of attacks on the Romans, harassing them perpetually, retarding their labors, and drawing their attention from that point of their line by which he purposed to extricate his army. At last, on a night when a terrible snowstorm was raging, he led his men to a place where the Roman works were yet incomplete, the snow enabling them to march noiselessly. When they reached the line, the immense ditches seemed to bar their further advance; but they set resolutely at work to fill them. Earth, snow, fagots, and dead bodies of men and beasts were hastily thrown into them; and across this singular bridge the whole army poured into the country, leaving the Roman camp behind, and having rendered nugatory all the laborious digging and trenching of the legions.

It was not until the next morning that Crassus discovered what had been done, and how thoroughly he had been outgeneralled by Spartacus. But he had no room for vexation in his mind. He was so frightened as a Roman citizen, that he could not feel mortified as a Roman soldier. He took counsel of his fears, and did that which he had cause both to be ashamed of and to regret in after days. He wrote to the Senate, stating that in his opinion not only should Pompeius be summoned home from Spain, but Lucullus also from the East, to aid in putting down an enemy who was unconquerable by ordinary means. A short time sufficed to show how indiscreetly for his own fame he had acted; for Spartacus was unable to follow up his success, in consequence of mutinies in his army. The Gauls again rebelled against his authority, and left him. Crassus concentrated his whole force in an attack on the seceders, and a battle followed which Plutarch says was the most severely contested of the war. The Romans remained masters of the field, more than twelve thousand of the Gauls being slain, of whom only two were wounded in the back, the rest falling in the ranks. Spartacus retreated to the mountains of Petelia, closely followed by Roman detachments. Turning upon them, he drove them back; but this last gleam of success led to his destruction. His policy was to avoid a battle, but his men would not listen to his prudent counsels, and compelled him to face about and march against Crassus. This was what the Roman desired; for Pompeius was bringing up an army from Spain, and would be sure to reap all the honors of the war, were it to be prolonged.

Some accounts represent Spartacus as anxious for battle. Whether he was so or not, he made every preparation that became a good general. The armies met on the Silarus, in the northern part of Lucania; and the battle which followed, and which was to finish this remarkable war, was fought not far from where the traveller now sees the noble ruins of Paestum. Spartacus made his last speech to his soldiers, warning them of what they would have to expect, if they should fall alive into the hands of their old masters. By way of practical commentary on his text, he caused a cross to be erected on a height, and to that cross was nailed a living Roman, whose agonies were visible to the whole army. Spartacus then ordered his horse to be brought to him in front of the army, and slew the animal with his own hands. "I am determined," he said to his men, "to share all your dangers. Our positions shall be the same. If we are victorious, I shall get horses enough from the foe. If we are beaten, I shall need a horse no more." The battle that followed was the most severely contested action of that warlike period, which, extending through two generations, saw the victories of Marius over the Northern barbarians at its commencement, and Pharsalia and Munda and Philippi at its close. The insurgents attacked with great fury, but with method, Spartacus leading the way at the head of a band of select followers, thus acting the part of a soldier as well as of a general. The Romans steadily resisted,—and the slaughter was great on both sides. At last, victory began to incline towards the gladiators, when Spartacus fell, and the fortune of the day was changed. He had made a fierce charge on the Romans, with the intention of cutting his way to Crassus. Two centurions had fallen by his sword, and a number of inferior men, when he was himself wounded in one of his thighs. Falling upon one knee, he still continued to fight, until he was overpowered and slain. The battle was maintained for some time longer, and ended only with the destruction of the insurgents, thirty thousand of whom were killed;—Livy puts their killed at forty thousand. The Roman slain numbered twenty thousand, and they had as many more wounded. Only six thousand prisoners fell into the hands of Crassus, who caused the whole of them to be crucified,—the crosses being placed at intervals on both sides of the Appian Way, between Capua and Rome, and the whole Roman army being marched through the horrible lines. A body of five thousand fugitives, who sought refuge in the north, were intercepted by Pompeius on his homeward march from Spain, and slaughtered to a man.

Thus fell Spartacus, and far more nobly than either of the great republican chiefs whose deaths were so soon to follow. Pompeius, who boasted that he had cut up the war by the roots, ran away from Pharsalia, without an effort to retrieve his fortunes, though the force opposed to him in the battle was only half as large as his own, and he had still abundant resources for future operations. Crassus, who claimed to have conquered Spartacus, and who not unreasonably resented the pretensions of Pompeius, fell miserably in Parthia, after having led the Romans to the most fatal of their fields except Cannæ. Wanting the nerve to die sword in hand in the midst of his foes, like Spartacus, he consented to adorn the triumph of those foes, and perished as ignominiously as the great gladiator gloriously.

(*The Atlantic Monthly*, 1858)

Spartacus' Speech

The speech below was written by a 19th-century author, imagining what the night of the uprising felt like, and what Spartacus said to rally his brothers-in-arms.

SPARTACUS: Ye call me chief; and ye do well to call him chief who for twelve long years has met upon the arena every shape of man or beast the broad Empire of Rome could furnish, and who never yet lowered his arm. If there be one among you who can say that ever, in public fight or private brawl, my actions did belie my tongue, let him stand forth and say it. If there be three in all your company dare face me on the bloody sands, let them come on. And yet I was not always thus,—a hired butcher, a savage chief of still more savage men. My ancestors came from old Sparta, and settled among the vine-clad rocks and citron groves of Syrasella. My early life ran quiet as the brooks by which I sported; and when, at noon, I gathered the sheep beneath the shade, and played upon the shepherd's flute, there was a friend, the son of a neighbor, to join me in the pastime. We led our flocks to the same pasture, and partook together our rustic meal. One evening, after the sheep were folded, and we were all seated beneath the myrtle which shaded our cottage, my grandsire, an old man, was telling of Marathon and Leuctra; and how, in ancient times, a little band of Spartans, in a defile of the mountains, had withstood a whole army. I did not then know what war was; but my cheeks burned, I know not why, and I clasped the knees of that venerable man, until my mother, parting the hair from off my forehead, kissed my throbbing temples, and bade me go to rest, and think no more of those old tales and savage wars. That very night the Romans landed on our coast. I saw the breast that had nourished me trampled by the hoof of the war-horse,—the bleeding body of my father flung amidst the blazing rafters of our dwelling! To-day I killed a man in the arena; and, when I broke his helmet-clasps, behold!

he was my friend. He knew me, smiled faintly, gasped, and died;—the same sweet smile upon his lips that I had marked, when, in adventurous boyhood, we scaled the lofty cliff to pluck the first ripe grapes, and bear them home in childish triumph! I told the prætor that the dead man had been my friend, generous and brave; and I begged that I might bear away the body, to burn it on a funeral pile, and mourn over its ashes. Ay! upon my knees, amid the dust and blood of the arena, I begged that poor boon, while all the assembled maids and matrons, and the holy virgins they call Vestals, and the rabble, shouted in derision, deeming it rare sport, forsooth, to see Rome's fiercest gladiator turn pale and tremble at the sight of that piece of bleeding clay! And the prætor drew back as I were pollution, and sternly said, "Let the carrion rot; there are no noble men but Romans." And so, fellow-gladiators, must you, and so must I, die like dogs. O Rome! Rome! thou hast been a tender nurse to me. Ay! thou hast given to that poor, gentle, timid shepherd lad, who never knew a harsher tone than a flute-note, muscles of iron and a heart of flint; taught him to drive the sword through plaited mail and links of rugged brass, and warm it in the marrow of his foe;—to gaze into the glaring eyeballs of the fierce Numidian lion, even as a boy upon a laughing girl! And he shall pay thee back, until the yellow Tiber is red as frothing wine, and in its deepest ooze thy life-blood lies curdled! Ye stand here now like giants, as ye are! The strength of brass is in your toughened sinews, but to-morrow some Roman Adonis, breathing sweet perfume from his curly locks, shall with his lily fingers pat your red brawn, and bet his sesterces upon your blood. Hark! hear ye yon lion roaring in his den? 'Tis three days since he has tasted flesh; but to-morrow he shall break his fast upon yours,—and a dainty meal for him ye will be! If ye are beasts, then stand here like fat oxen, waiting for the butcher's knife! If ye are men, follow me! Strike down yon guard, gain the mountain passes, and there do bloody work, as did your sires at old Thermopylæ! Is Sparta dead? Is the old Grecian spirit frozen in your veins, that you do crouch and cower like a belabored hound beneath his master's lash? O comrades! warriors! Thracians! if we must fight, let us fight for ourselves! If we must slaughter, let us slaughter our oppressors! If we must die, let it be under the clear sky, by the bright waters, in noble, honorable battle!

(Kellogg, 1842)

COMMODUS

A Collection of Writings

COMMODUS, LUCIUS AELIUS AURELIUS (161–192), also called Marcus Antoninus, emperor of Rome, son of Marcus Aurelius and Faustina, was born at Lanuvium on the 31st of August 161. In spite of a careful education he soon showed a fondness for low society and amusement. At the age of fifteen he was associated by his father in the government. On the death of Aurelius, whom he had accompanied in the war against the Quadi and Marcomanni, he hastily concluded peace and hurried back to Rome. The first years of his reign were uneventful, but in 183 he was attacked by an assassin at the instigation of his sister Lucilla and many members of the senate, which felt deeply insulted by the contemptuous manner in which Commodus treated it. From this time he became tyrannical.

Many distinguished Romans were put to death as implicated in the conspiracy, and others were executed for no reason at all. The treasury was exhausted by lavish expenditure on gladiatorial and wild beast combats and on the soldiery, and the property of the wealthy was confiscated. At the same time Commodus, proud of his bodily strength and dexterity, exhibited himself in the arena, slew wild animals and fought with gladiators, and commanded that he should be worshipped as the Roman Hercules. Plots against his life naturally began to spring up. That of his favourite Perennis, praefect of the praetorian guard, was discovered in time.

The next danger was from the people, who were infuriated by the dearth of corn. The mob repelled the praetorian guard, but the execution of the hated minister Cleander quieted the tumult. The attempt also of the daring highwayman Maternus to seize the empire was betrayed; but at last Eclectus the emperor's chamberlain, Laetus the praefect of the praetorians, and his mistress Marcia, finding their names on the list of those doomed to death, united to destroy him. He was poisoned, and then strangled by a wrestler named Narcissus, on the 31st of December 192. During his reign unimportant wars were successfully carried on by his generals Clodius Albinus, Pescennius Niger and Ulpius Marcellus. The frontier of Dacia was successfully defended against the Scythians and Sarmatians, and a tract of territory reconquered in north Britain.

In 1874 a statue of Commodus was dug up at Rome, in which he is represented as Hercules—a lion's skin on his head, a club in his right and the apples of the Hesperides in his left hand.

(*Encyclopædia Britannica*, 1911)

During the later Roman Empire, Commodus, in the degenerate days of Rome, at great expense had wild beasts brought from distant lands that he might have the glory of slaying them in the Roman circus; and medals representing himself as Hercules slaying the Nemean lion were struck at his orders.

(Schreiner, 1911)

The Cruelty, Follies and Murder of Commodus

The monstrous vices of the son have cast a shade on the purity of the father's virtues. It has been objected to Marcus, that he sacrificed the happiness of millions to a fond partiality for a worthless boy; and that he chose a successor in his own family, rather than in the republic. Nothing however, was neglected by the anxious father, and by the men of virtue and learning whom he summoned to his assistance, to expand the narrow mind of young Commodus, to correct his growing vices, and to render him worthy of the throne for which he was designed. But the power of instruction is seldom of much efficacy, except in those happy dispositions where it is almost superfluous. The distasteful lesson of a grave philosopher was, in a moment, obliterated by the whisper of a profligate favorite; and Marcus himself blasted the fruits of this labored education, by admitting his son, at the age of fourteen or fifteen, to a full participation of the Imperial power. He lived but four years afterwards: but he lived long enough to repent a rash measure, which raised the impetuous youth above the restraint of reason and authority.

(...)

Yet Commodus was not, as he has been represented, a tiger born with an insatiate thirst of human blood, and capable, from his infancy, of the most inhuman actions. Nature had formed him of a weak rather than a wicked disposition. His simplicity and timidity rendered him the slave of his attendants, who gradually corrupted his mind. His cruelty, which at first obeyed the dictates of others, degenerated into habit, and at length became the ruling passion of his soul.

Upon the death of his father, Commodus found himself embarrassed with the command of a great army, and the conduct of a difficult war against the Quadi and Marcomanni. The servile and profligate youths whom Marcus had banished, soon regained their station and influence about the new emperor. They exaggerated the hardships and dangers of a campaign in the wild countries beyond the Danube; and they assured the indolent prince that the terror of his name, and the arms of his lieutenants, would be sufficient to complete the conquest of the dismayed barbarians, or to impose such conditions as were more advantageous than any conquest. By a dexterous application to his sensual appetites, they compared the tranquillity, the splendor, the refined pleasures of Rome, with the tumult of a Pannonian camp, which afforded neither leisure nor materials for luxury. Commodus listened to the pleasing advice; but whilst he hesitated between his own inclination and the awe which he still retained for his father's counsellors, the summer insensibly elapsed, and his triumphal entry into the capital was deferred till the autumn. His graceful person, popular address, and imagined virtues, attracted the public favor; the honorable peace which he had recently granted to the barbarians, diffused a universal joy; his impatience to revisit Rome was fondly ascribed to the love of his country; and his dissolute course of amusements was faintly condemned in a prince of nineteen years of age.

One evening, as the emperor was returning to the palace, through a dark and narrow portico in the amphitheatre, an assassin, who waited his passage, rushed upon him with a drawn sword, loudly exclaiming, "*The senate sends you this.*" The menace prevented the deed; the assassin was seized by the guards, and immediately revealed the authors of the conspiracy. It had been formed, not in the state, but within the walls of the palace. Lucilla, the emperor's sister, and widow of Lucius Verus, impatient of the second rank, and jealous of the reigning empress, had armed the murderer against her brother's life. She had not ventured to communicate the black design to her second husband, Claudius Pompeiarus, a senator of distinguished merit and unshaken loyalty; but among the crowd of her lovers (for she imitated the manners of Faustina) she found men of desperate fortunes and wild ambition, who were prepared to serve her more violent, as well as her tender passions. The conspirators experienced the rigor of justice, and the abandoned princess was punished, first with exile, and afterwards with death.

But the words of the assassin sunk deep into the mind of Commodus, and left an indelible impression of fear and hatred against the whole body of the senate.[*] Those whom he had dreaded as importunate ministers, he now suspected as secret enemies.

Every sentiment of virtue and humanity was extinct in the mind of Commodus. Whilst he thus abandoned the reins of empire to these unworthy favorites, he valued nothing in sovereign power, except the unbounded license of indulging his sensual

---

[*] The conspirators were senators, even the assassin himself. Herod. 81.

appetites. His hours were spent in a seraglio of three hundred beautiful women, and as many boys, of every rank, and of every province; and, wherever the arts of seduction proved ineffectual, the brutal lover had recourse to violence. The ancient historians have expatiated on these abandoned scenes of prostitution, which scorned every restraint of nature or modesty; but it would not be easy to translate their too faithful descriptions into the decency of modern language. The intervals of lust were filled up with the basest amusements. The influence of a polite age, and the labor of an attentive education, had never been able to infuse into his rude and brutish mind the least tincture of learning; and he was the first of the Roman emperors totally devoid of taste for the pleasures of the understanding. Nero himself excelled, or affected to excel, in the elegant arts of music and poetry: nor should we despise his pursuits, had he not converted the pleasing relaxation of a leisure hour into the serious business and ambition of his life. But Commodus, from his earliest infancy, discovered an aversion to whatever was rational or liberal, and a fond attachment to the amusements of the populace; the sports of the circus and amphitheatre, the combats of gladiators, and the hunting of wild beasts. The masters in every branch of learning, whom Marcus provided for his son, were heard with inattention and disgust; whilst the Moors and Parthians, who taught him to dart the javelin and to shoot with the bow, found a disciple who delighted in his application, and soon equalled the most skilful of his instructors in the steadiness of the eye and the dexterity of the hand.

The servile crowd, whose fortune depended on their master's vices, applauded these ignoble pursuits. The perfidious voice of flattery reminded him, that by exploits of the same nature, by the defeat of the Nemæan lion, and the slaughter of the wild boar of Erymanthus, the Grecian Hercules had acquired a place among the gods, and an immortal memory among men. They only forgot to observe, that, in the first ages of society, when the fiercer animals often dispute with man the possession of an unsettled country, a successful war against those savages is one of the most innocent and beneficial labours of heroism. In the civilized state of the Roman empire, the wild beasts had long since retired from the face of man, and the neighbourhood of populous cities. To surprise them in their solitary haunts, and to transport them to Rome, that they might be slain in pomp by the hand of an emperor, was an enterprise equally ridiculous for the prince and oppressive for the people.[*] Ignorant of these distinctions, Commodus eagerly embraced the glorious resemblance, and styled himself (as we still read on his medals) the *Roman Hercules*.[†] The club and the lion's hide were placed by the side of the throne, amongst the ensigns of sovereignty; and statues were erected, in which Commodus was represented in the character, and with the attributes, of the god, whose valor and dexterity he endeavored to emulate in the daily course of his ferocious amusements.

Elated with these praises, which gradually extinguished the innate sense of shame, Commodus resolved to exhibit before the eyes of the Roman people those exercises, which till then he had decently confined within the walls of his palace, and to the presence of a few favorites. On the appointed day, the various motives of flattery, fear, and curiosity, attracted to the

---

[*] The African lions, when pressed by hunger, infested the open villages and cultivated country; and they infested them with impunity. The royal beast was reserved for the pleasures of the emperor and the capital; and the unfortunate peasant who killed one of them though in his own defence, incurred a very heavy penalty. This extraordinary game-law was mitigated by Honorius, and finally repealed by Justinian.

[†] Commodus placed his own head on the colossal statue of Hercules with the inscription, Lucius Commodus Hercules. The wits of Rome, according to a new fragment of Dion, published an epigram, of which, like many other ancient jests, the point is not very clear. It seems to be a protest of the god against being confounded with the emperor.

amphitheatre an innumerable multitude of spectators; and some degree of applause was deservedly bestowed on the uncommon skill of the Imperial performer. Whether he aimed at the head or heart of the animal, the wound was alike certain and mortal. With arrows whose point was shaped into the form of crescent, Commodus often intercepted the rapid career, and cut asunder the long, bony neck of the ostrich. A panther was let loose; and the archer waited till he had leaped upon a trembling malefactor. In the same instant the shaft flew, the beast dropped dead, and the man remained unhurt. The dens of the amphitheatre disgorged at once a hundred lions: a hundred darts from the unerring hand of Commodus laid them dead as they run raging round the *Arena*. Neither the huge bulk of the elephant, nor the scaly hide of the rhinoceros, could defend them from his stroke. Æthiopia and India yielded their most extraordinary productions; and several animals were slain in the amphitheatre, which had been seen only in the representations of art, or perhaps of fancy. In all these exhibitions, the securest precautions were used to protect the person of the Roman Hercules from the desperate spring of any savage, who might possibly disregard the dignity of the emperor and the sanctity of the god.

But the meanest of the populace were affected with shame and indignation when they beheld their sovereign enter the lists as a gladiator, and glory in a profession which the laws and manners of the Romans had branded with the justest note of infamy.[*] He chose the habit and arms of the *Secutor*, whose combat with the *Retiarius* formed one of the most lively scenes in the bloody sports of the amphitheatre. The *Secutor* was armed with a helmet, sword, and buckler; his naked antagonist had only a large net

---

[*] The virtuous and even the wise princes forbade the senators and knights to embrace this scandalous profession, under pain of infamy, or, what was more dreaded by those profligate wretches, of exile. The tyrants allured them to dishonor by threats and rewards. Nero once produced in the arena forty senators and sixty knights.

and a trident; with the one he endeavored to entangle, with the other to despatch his enemy. If he missed the first throw, he was obliged to fly from the pursuit of the *Secutor*, till he had prepared his net for a second cast. The emperor fought in this character seven hundred and thirty-five several times. These glorious achievements were carefully recorded in the public acts of the empire; and that he might omit no circumstance of infamy, he received from the common fund of gladiators a stipend so exorbitant that it became a new and most ignominious tax upon the Roman people. It may be easily supposed, that in these engagements the master of the world was always successful; in the amphitheatre, his victories were not often sanguinary; but when he exercised his skill in the school of gladiators, or his own palace, his antagonists were frequently honoured with a mortal wound from the hand of Commodus, and obliged to seal their flattery with their blood.* He now disdained the appellation of Hercules. The name of Paulus, a celebrated Secutor, was the only one which delighted his ear. It was inscribed on his colossal statues, and repeated in the redoubled acclamations of the mournful and applauding senate. Claudius Pompeianus, the virtuous husband of Lucilla, was the only senator who asserted the honor of his rank. As a father, he permitted his sons to consult their safety by attending the amphitheatre. As a Roman, he declared, that his own life was in the emperor's hands, but that he would never behold the son of Marcus prostituting his person and dignity. Notwithstanding his manly resolution Pompeianus escaped the resentment of the tyrant, and, with his honour, had the good fortune to preserve his life.

Commodus had now attained the summit of vice and infamy. Amidst the acclamations of a flattering court, he was unable to disguise from himself, that he had deserved the contempt and hatred of every man of sense and virtue in his empire. His

---

* Victor tells us, that Commodus only allowed his antagonists a . . . weapon, dreading most probably the consequences of their despair.

ferocious spirit was irritated by the consciousness of that hatred, by the envy of every kind of merit, by the just apprehension of danger, and by the habit of slaughter, which he contracted in his daily amusements. History has preserved a long list of consular senators sacrificed to his wanton suspicion, which sought out, with peculiar anxiety, those unfortunate persons connected, however remotely, with the family of the Antonines, without sparing even the ministers of his crimes or pleasures. His cruelty proved at last fatal to himself. He had shed with impunity the noblest blood of Rome: he perished as soon as he was dreaded by his own domestics. Marcia, his favorite concubine, Eclectus, his chamberlain, and Lætus, his Prætorian præfect, alarmed by the fate of their companions and predecessors, resolved to prevent the destruction which every hour hung over their heads, either from the mad caprice of the tyrant, or the sudden indignation of the people. Marcia seized the occasion of presenting a draught of wine to her lover, after he had fatigued himself with hunting some wild beasts. Commodus retired to sleep; but whilst he was labouring with the effects of poison and drunkenness, a robust youth, by profession a wrestler, entered his chamber, and strangled him without resistance. The body was secretly conveyed out of the palace, before the least suspicion was entertained in the city, or even in the court, of the emperor's death. Such was the fate of the son of Marcus, and so easy was it to destroy a hated tyrant, who, by the artificial powers of government, had oppressed, during thirteen years, so many millions of subjects, each of whom was equal to their master in personal strength and personal abilities.

(Gibbon, 1845)

PRISCUS AND VERUS

Fragments in History

Gladiators were generally matched in pairs. It was ordinarily expected that the fight would be to a finish, i.e. until one of the combatants, by dropping his weapon and raising his hand, if able to do so, begged for mercy. The conditions of the combat (*lex*, 4-5) were announced before the fight began. In this fight Priscus and Verus were so evenly matched that neither could gain the mastery. Hence neither appealed for *missio*, i.e. for mercy and discharge from further service for that day.—*Meter: §48*

(Martial, 1908)

While Verus and Priscus were prolonging the combat, and the valour of each had been for a long time equal, quarter for the combatants was demanded with great clamour. But Caesar obeyed his own law. The law was to fight with a stated reward in view, till by his thumb one of the pair proclaimed himself vanquished: but, as was allowed, he frequently gave them dishes and gifts. An end, however, was found for the well-matched contest: equal they fought, equal they resigned. Caesar sent wands to each, to each the meed of victory. Such was the reward that adroit valour received. Under no other prince save thee, Caesar, has this ever happened, that, when two fought with each other, both were victors.

SAVAGERY IN SANDALS

When Priscus, Verus, did prolong their fight,
Characterized by Mars with equal spite,
For their discharge a joint consent applied
Itself to Caesar; by whom't was denied.
It was the fashion so long to contend
Till the vanquish'd made signs the fight should end:
And to detain the people to the last,
Gifts were provided, and a slight repast.
Even wounds the sword-players did engrave;
They fought alike; or equal scores did leave.
Caesar acquitted both, gave both the palm:
Thus prowess for her cure acquired a balm.
Before your reign, Caesar, who thought to see,
When champions fight, that both should victors be?
                                         —*Pecke.*

(Martial, 1890)

HERMES

Fragments in History

Hermes is the pride of his age in martial contests; Hermes is skilled in all kinds of arms; Hermes is a gladiator and a master of gladiators; Hermes is the terror and awe of his whole school; Hermes is he of whom alone Helius is afraid; Hermes is he to whom alone Advolans submits; Hermes is skilled in conquering without a blow; Hermes is his own body of reserve;* Hermes makes the fortunes of the letters of seats; Hermes is the object of care and anxiety to the actresses; Hermes walks proudly with the warlike spear; Hermes threatens with Neptune's trident; Hermes is terrible with the helmet shading the face; Hermes is the glory of Mars in every way; Hermes is everything in himself, and thrice a man.†

---

* Other gladiators were succeeded by fresh ones, when they were tired; Hermes was never tired.

† In allusion to Hermes Trismegistus. This Hermes is as great in the arena as the other was in science.

SAVAGERY IN SANDALS

Hermes, the martial glory of the age,
Skilful in all the combats of the stage;
Hermes, master of fence, and fencer too;
The cock and terror of the sword-men's crew;
Hermes, whom Helius fears, but fears alone,
Advolans yields to, yet to him but one;
Hermes, that knows to conquer without blows,
The second to himself against all foes;
Hermes, the stage's mint and endless gain,
The love and strife of all their female train;
Hermes, that proudly shakes the warlike spear,
And fiercely threat'ning does the trident bear;
Hermes, when casked for the blindfold fight,
When moped and drooping seems, does then afiright;
Hermes engrosses all men's gifts in one,
And Trismegistus' name deserves alone.
—*Anon*, 1695.
(Martial, 1890)

BIBLIOGRAPHY

Blake, W.O. (1861) *The History of Slavery and the Slave Trade, Ancient and Modern: The Forms of Slavery that Prevailed in Ancient Nations, Particularly in Greece and Rome.* Columbus, Ohio: H. Miller.

Cicero, M.T. and Yonge, C.D. (1851) *The Orations of Marcus Tullius Cicero.* London: H.G. Bohn.

Eisen, G.A. (1927) *Glass: Its Origin, History, Chronology, Technic and Classification to the Sixteenth Century.* New York: W.E. Rudge.

Encyclopædia Britannica (1911). Volume 6. Cambridge, England: University Press.

Encyclopædia Britannica (1911). Volume 12. Cambridge, England: University Press.

Garnett, R.E. (1899) *The International Library of Famous Literature.* London: The Standard.

Gérôme, J.L. (1872) 'Pollice Verso (Thumbs Down).' (Oil on canvas).

Gérôme, J.L. (19th century) 'A Retiarius.' (Oil on panel).

Gibbon, E. (1845) *The History of the Decline and Fall of the Roman Empire.* Edited by H.H. Milman. Philadelphia: Porter & Coates.

Hemans, F. (1812) *The Domestic Affections, and Other Poems.* London: T. Cadell, and W. Davies.

Hering, F.F. (1892) *Gérôme: The Life and Works of Jean Léon Gérôme*. New York: Cassell Publishing Company.

Johnston, H.W. (1903) *The Private Life of the Romans*. Chicago: Scott, Foresman and Company.

Jones, H.S. (1912) *Companion to Roman History*. Oxford: Clarendon Press.

Juvenalis, D.J. and Flaccus, A.P. (1918) *Juvenal and Persius*. Translated by G.G. Ramsay. London: William Heinemann.

Kellogg, E. (1842) 'Spartacus to the Gladiators at Capua'. Brunswick, Maine.

Martial, M.V. (1890) *The Epigrams of Martial*. Translated by H.G. Bohn. London: G. Bell and Sons.

Martial, M.V. (1908) *Selected Epigrams of Martial*. Edited by E. Post. USA: Ginn and Company.

Morris, C. (1896) *Historic Tales; The Romance of Reality*. Philadelphia and London: J. B. Lippincott Company.

Naso, P.O. (1930) *The Love Books of Ovid; Being the Amores, Ars Amatoria, Remedia Amoris and Medicamina Faciei Femineae of Publius Ovidius Naso*. Translated by J.L. May. New York: Rarity Press.

Schreiner, O. (1911) *Woman and Labor*. New York: Frederick A. Stokes Company.

Seneca, L.A. (1917) *Epistulae morales ad Lucilium (Moral letters to Lucilius)*. Translated by R.M. Gummere. London: William Heinemann.

The Atlantic Monthly (1858) 'Spartacus', January.

Thomas, E. (1899) *Roman Life Under the Caesars.* New York & London: G.P. Putnam's Sons.

Wiseman, N.P. (1863) *Points of Contact Between Science and Art: A Lecture Delivered at the Royal Institution, January* 30, 1863. London: Hurst and Blackett.

Yaggy, L.W. and Haines, T.L. (1880) *Museum of Antiquity; A Description of Ancient Life.* Chicago: Western Publishing House.

Printed in Great Britain
by Amazon